Michael Beckett was born in Essex and married at the age of 21 to Debbie. They have four grown-up children who each have two children. They have lived half their lives in Cambridge following Michael's ordination into the Church of England in 1988. He was vicar of St Paul's Church in Cambridge for 28 years and retired in the year 2021. He already has one book published, *The Gospel in Esther*.

My Special friend
Who be stand to gour
Lets me all there year
Thankyou

Michael.

This book is dedicated to the people with whom I have shared my personal journey of all these years in Cambridge and to the people of the St Paul's family, both to those who attend on a Sunday and those who do not.

Michael Beckett

AUTHENTIC CHURCH

A radically old model of being
church for twenty first
century Britain

AUSTIN MACAULEY PUBLISHERS™
LONDON • CAMBRIDGE • NEW YORK • SHARJAH

A CIP catalogue record for this title is available from the British Library.

ISBN 9781398424340 (Paperback)
ISBN 9781398437289 (ePub e-book)

www.austinmacauley.com

First Published 2022
Austin Macauley Publishers Ltd®
1 Canada Square
Canary Wharf
London
E14 5AA

I would like to thank the PCC of St Paul's for giving me the time and the opportunity to write this, the St Paul's family for their love and encouragement, my long-suffering wife without whose wisdom I would not be the person that I am and to my editor, Lesley Thomas, who ordered my stream of consciousness into a readable form.

Foreword

Michael Beckett is the kind of priest that only the Church of England could have produced; someone who serves everyone in his parish and particularly those disregarded by society. This book is the fruit of nearly thirty years of ministry at St Paul's, Cambridge, a church that seeks to proclaim a radically inclusive vision of the Gospel, and from which significant ministry among street-homeless people in the city is based. I have publicly called St Paul's the most beautiful church community in Cambridge for its welcome of the dispossessed. Former Archbishop of Canterbury Rowan Williams once said that for Jesus, the centre is on the edge. And it is this conviction that underlies the vision of the Church that Michael expounds in this book, which offers an extended theological reflection on what it might mean to be the Church today. This represents something of his own journey from mainstream conservative evangelicalism to a living a radical gospel of diversity and strength in vulnerability.

This text reminds me of Albert Nolan's book, *Jesus Before Christianity*, not because they are similarly written but because both works are very orthodox in their radicalism, drawing upon the witness of the first Christians as represented in the Acts of the Apostles. Michael's ecclesiology is rooted in deep engagement with the text of Scripture, handling it with care and interrogating it for its meaning for the Church today. Again, and again, he comes back to just how radical Jesus and his teaching were, and just how radical the earliest Christian community or fellowship was, beginning with an exposition of Acts 2:42. This conviction frames Michael's argument, as he explores four 'foundational pillars' of the early Christians' experience of the risen Lord and the way they lived in response. He takes us through what he describes as 'the early Church's experience of refashioning humanity in the light of Jesus', as they met together, read Scripture, broke bread, and prayed. This last is expanded in the later chapters focussing on prayer in general, and then specifically on the Lord's Prayer. Michael shows us how all of these were differently prophetic, variously justice-oriented, and so point to a way of thinking about what it means to be the Church that challenges many of our received understandings. Michael is driven by reflective practice and holy curiosity. His understanding of the Eucharist and its power and purpose have changed dramatically in recent years. The Church gathering for the Eucharist is seen more like a multi-generational family meal; true Christian fellowship bears many of the characteristics of an Alcoholics Anonymous meeting, in its depth of 'non-judgement and acceptance, authenticity, honesty and vulnerability'.

The vision of the Church, and the vision of the Kingdom, presented in this book are prophetic. Michael is an uncomfortable if wonderful friend for a bishop: there is some trenchant critique of the Church's collusion with worldly power, with exclusion, and with abuse. But this is a profoundly hopeful book – calling us back to the radical, life-changing, world-changing simplicity that the earliest Christians lived as they lived their response to the life-transforming, world-transforming life, death, and resurrection of Jesus Christ. This is a heartfelt call to the Church to learn of Christ as true disciples, to be shaped more profoundly by the words of Scripture, and to be ever more attentive to those who are marginalised and excluded today. It is a vivid and compelling picture of the possibilities of Church and world shaped in authentic response to the God who in Christ kneels and washes feet before being lifted up to draw all people to himself.

It is, as the quotation with which Michael ends has it, a vision of the Church where nothing at all matters but God's love. It is a book that invites us to wonder, to wish, to ask, and then challenges us, to go, to speak, and to act in ways that witness to that love.

– The Rt Revd Stephen Conway
The Bishop of Ely

Introduction

I shall attempt in this book to outline what were the four foundational pillars of the early Church's experience of the risen LORD and their devotion thereto. This emerging church fellowship was the 'natural' expression or outworking of what it was that had so destabilised them and wrought such a change in their view of themselves, their neighbours, their world and indeed of their God.

Those who made up that company would in those early days all have been Jewish. Thus the lens through which they read that experience was that of their Hebrew scriptures, reinterpreted to them and for them both by the Apostles, who had accompanied Jesus for three years on earth, and by the Holy Spirit, whom Jesus had promised to send to lead them into all truth.

How radical this experience would have been is almost impossible for us to grasp, and this will be the subject of **chapter 3**, the fellowship to which these early followers in the way, devoted themselves, in the light of the Apostles' teaching. As a fellowship they wanted to express their continuity with the religion of their birth and at the same time a radical discontinuity. Hence they chose the word ecclesia from their Hebrew scriptures to describe their early gatherings. It was one of two words used in their Hebrew scriptures to describe the assembly of God's people. The other was sunagos, which was already the word used to describe the gatherings of their fellow Jews and therefore inappropriate for this nascent sect.

In the light of the Apostles' teaching this early fellowship regarded Jesus as the person who had appeared to the people of God throughout their history and as recorded in their Hebrew scriptures in the person of Yahweh, translated as Lord. This was of course utter blasphemy to those who did not receive the Apostles' preaching and who remained loyal to the religion of their birth. But "Jesus is Lord" became THE article of faith of this early fellowship or church as the Apostle Paul's writing makes clear (Rom 12:3). As a result, this early fellowship was not only at odds with the Judaism of its day, but also with the Roman Empire in which they lived and breathed and had their being, which viewed the Emperor as the Son of God and the Lord.

I recently watched a series on the TV which told the story of a young person attempting to 'escape' from the closed religious sect that she had grown up in. Her experience of the 'outside world' was for her at one and the same time shocking and liberating. There was one particular moment when she realised that she had been given something to eat that her strict upbringing disallowed. She immediately went outside preparing herself to be sick. She was not, and it was in that moment that she had something of an Epiphany.

She realised that what she had been told all her life would happen had not. It was at best a construction and at worst a lie, a tool, a means to maintain conformity to a 'closed-community' way of being, that had the benefit of security and the limitation of imprisonment. Having longed for more, for freedom, for the opportunity to be herself, to think for herself, to simply question, she felt compelled to 'escape', as heart-breaking as that was, to leave those whom she loved. And this was precisely the experience of that early Church fellowship.

Jesus confounded expectations almost all the time during his time on Earth, culturally, socially and especially religiously. On one occasion, having been touched by a woman in public the religious leaders are angered and question his authority and his calling as a prophet. How he could allow such a thing, surely he would know "what kind of woman she was?" Separation from the wider culture, from Gentile "dogs" and the exclusivity of the community not only as regards outsiders but also insiders who were deemed unclean and untouchable, and of which there were numerous categories within a very clearly laid out hierarchy, was the order of the day, the guardians of which were inevitably educated males.

Yet here was Jesus with his obvious popular appeal, together with his inverting interpretation of their Scriptures, being touched by the unclean, associating with women in public, eating with "sinners", going, even to the home of a quisling, a tax collector, deemed the very worst amongst them, and all this openly, unashamedly and deliberately provoking them to outrage. It was no wonder that a way needed to be found to be rid of him, one who was such a threat to their world view, to their security, to their socially constructed patriarchy.

Thus in that chapter we shall explore in a little more depth the radical nature of the break with the religion of their birth and the stance they took against the values not only of that religion but of wider society. We shall suggest that not only was their fellowship radically open to those within their own religion who would have been viewed as unclean but also to Gentiles, foreigners, pagans who also would have been viewed as unclean.

We shall explore this through the lens of the family meal table at which several generations gather, with conflicting agendas, needs and wants, acknowledging the reality of the messiness of such gatherings as well as that all members of the family are welcome whatever their age, ability, background, accomplishment, skin colour, gender or sexual orientation.

We shall acknowledge that such a fellowship has more in common with an AA meeting, with its level of non-judgement and acceptance, authenticity, honesty and vulnerability than most contemporary church services. And we shall attempt in line with the Apostles' teaching to reconfigure such words as orthodoxy, religion and liturgy in such a way as to make it clear that what that early Church fellowship sought to incarnate, was rooted in the model of Jesus' table fellowship when he was on Earth, in which he honoured the least and gave them greater honour than those who thought they were important, much to the chagrin of the latter. An order that reflected Jesus' reversal of normally understood and practised values, rather than some stratified formal gathering at the host of an elite householder, or the synagogue gatherings, dominated as they were by educated males, or the Roman households in which the majority were slaves and without rights or even a place at the table of their Lord and master.

Their gatherings therefore, would need to be completely reconstructed from their experience of Synagogue and

Temple. The strict divisions, between male and female, clean and unclean, priest and lay, not to mention their former utter exclusion of Gentiles, would all need to be abandoned. They were seeking to model themselves on Jesus' table fellowship which was inclusive of all peoples of whatever estate, as equally to be regarded as human beings and worthy of honour, as equally beloved of their heavenly Father and indeed as an expression of humanity, rather than of a particular or new religion. Jesus did not seek to establish a new religion and nor did they. This would all of course be messy, painful and take some time. The letters in the New Testament are an eloquent testimony to the challenges that early Church fellowship faced.

Some of these challenges will be the subject matter of our **first chapter** in which we will look at the commitment and devotion that characterised that early Church fellowship. The inclusion of unclean Jews was challenge enough as the number of Jewish followers grew, but with the experience of Saul on the road to Damascus of that same risen LORD, followed by his specific calling to be Paul the Apostle to the Gentiles, meant that the conflict that followed was almost inevitable.

This was manifest in two ways, first, between those who, rooted in their Hebrew religion and its socially constructed patriarchal way of being, regarded themselves as the acceptable, the righteous, the clean, and those newly liberated by Jesus within that religion who, until then, had always been told to regard themselves as unrighteous, unclean, and therefore marginalised, unacceptable and unwelcome in the synagogue and certainly in the Temple worship. This conflict of course finally flowered into the split between what would become known as the two religions of Christianity and Judaism, when the fulfilment of Jesus' prophecy of the destruction of Jerusalem and its temple occurred in AD 70.

Second, there was of course inevitable friction and disagreement between this new Hebrew sect within Judaism, that was learning to be inclusive and egalitarian, seeking to 'follow' in the footsteps of Jesus, the model and pioneer of their new faith, and those Gentiles who had also responded to the preaching of the Apostles. For to these new Gentile followers, the Law of Moses would have been largely unknown and most assuredly have had no day to day practical impact in their lives, the freedom from which the Apostle Paul dared, most shockingly of all, to confirm. These were indeed challenging, fraught and conflictual times, one might be tempted to say not unlike our own!

For not only was this early sect, as it sought to model itself upon Jesus' table fellowship, seeking to be non-judgemental, it was also learning to work out its patterns of relationship within its fellowship and with its neighbours without prescription, without laws, with a whole new set of cultural and socially constructed norms, which would enable its members to express individually and collectively, their trust and dependence upon the presence of the Risen Christ in their midst.

This was indeed most challenging and utterly destabilising for all its members and it is, as I say, almost impossible for us to have an appropriate grasp of its proportion. It was like an earthquake in their experience, as the rug of all that they had known about how to relate to one another was pulled from under their feet, individually and collectively. Thus in our first chapter we will give some consideration to who these people were and the dimensions of their struggle, and especially to their devotion to being an inclusive and open fellowship, rather than a closed sectarian one.

In **chapter 2** we shall turn our attention to the Apostles' teaching within that conflictual context. For not only were they working out the implications as well as explications of what Jesus had done, but they were also working out who it was that Jesus was. For very quickly they began to appreciate that Jesus was an even greater revelation of both divinity and humanity than ever they could have realised, prior to his resurrection that first Easter Sunday morning and that the breath of the Holy Spirit they received from Jesus in that upper room according to John and on the day of Pentecost according to Luke, was an extraordinary gift.

According to Luke, in the final climactic chapter of his Gospel, two disciples on the road to Emmaus were privileged to listen to the risen Lord Jesus open their Scriptures in such a way that their hearts burned within them. We shall attempt something of a reconstruction of that Bible study to which they were privileged that first Easter Sunday evening.

For Jesus was not merely or only their pioneer, their model and the fullest expression of what it means to be truly human, He was also the one who it turned out was the LORD, THE person who had appeared throughout Ancient Israel's history, as recorded in the Hebrew Scriptures, to various persons and in various circumstances, to warn, judge, comfort, console and guide His chosen people. A people whom he had called to be a light to and for the nations and yet who had not only so failed throughout their history to be such a light, but who also, and so misguidedly and so determinedly, chose to view themselves as privileged and set over and against those very nations.

But according to the Apostolic testimony as now recorded for us in what we call the New Testament, it was Jesus whom Isaiah had seen high and lifted up and whose glory filled the whole Temple, representing as they believed it did, the whole of creation (John 12:41). It was Jesus who was the beginning and the end (Rev. 1:17 et al), the One in whom all things in all creation hold together (Col. 1:17) The same Jesus who in conversation with Nicodemus says that He is the bronze serpent that Moses lifted up in the wilderness for the healing of his people (Numbers 21:8/9 & John 3:14) and who later expands the scope of that healing beyond ancient Israel, to include all peoples, when He is lifted up on the Cross (John 12:32).

It was their Father Abraham, whom the Apostle Paul would daringly proclaim was not merely their forefather, but the Father of all nations, just as God had promised he would be (Gen.17:4/Rom. 4:16), whom Jesus dares to suggest had seen his day (John 8:56). It was Jesus who revealed himself to Moses as the 'I AM' and whom John, in his Gospel, deliberately and provocatively, to the religion which gave him birth suggests, is revealed in the person of Jesus (Ex.3:14/John 6:35 et al). It was Jesus who was their great High Priest in the order of Melchizedek (Heb. 5:6) and who was also the final atoning sacrificial victim (Heb. 9:12). It was Jesus who was the One who entered the Holy of Holies bearing the sins of his people (Lev. 16/Isaiah 52:13-53:12), and emerged bearing the Name (Ps. 118:26/Luke 19:38).

Thus these early followers with the guidance of their Apostles, the Holy Spirit and Her testimony within them, wrestled to articulate their experience of the risen Lord and record it for us, so that in each new generation we can do the same. They did so from within the Hebrew religion and therefore it behoves us who are Gentile, to work hard to recover their reinterpretation of what their Hebrew Scriptures were now saying to them rather than what they *seemed* to have been saying for generations.

For now, in Jesus these Scriptures had been fulfilled in the most unexpected ways and required reinterpretation again and again. And it was this experience of those two disciples on the road to Emmaus that first Easter Sunday that we shall try to recapture in chapter 2, so that we may emulate that early Church fellowship in reinterpreting those same Scriptures anew for our day and our generation.

In **chapter 4** we shall look at the central expression of that fellowship in the breaking of bread, the importance of which cannot be understated. For according to Luke's account of the experience of those two disciples who invite Jesus into their home, having journeyed with him on the road to Emmaus that first Easter Sunday evening, it was as Jesus broke the bread that their eyes were opened to 'see' who He truly was (Luke 24:31) Thus according to Luke, it is the Apostles' teaching and the breaking of bread that are the keys to opening eyes to Jesus.

So the early Church, that sect within the Judaism of its day, were seeking, as they gathered, to replicate the experience of those two disciples. And in addition we shall attempt to show that the primary way in which the Apostles interpreted that experience and that meal was not through the lens of the Passover, the actual context in which Jesus instituted the sacrament, but rather that of the annual day of 'at-one-ment', as prescribed in the book of Leviticus and fulfilled, or so it was anticipated, through the experience of the suffering servant, described in the servant songs of Isaiah, and to which the new Testament writers turn again and again.

I shall be conflicted as to whether or not to refer to the Lord's table as just that, a table, or as an altar, at which Jesus our great High Priest offers himself, the once and for all, the full and final, sacrificial victim. For as His actions are replicated by the priest on behalf of those who gather around that table, His name is invoked and His presence is bidden, that the bread and wine might be to us his body and his blood, the mystical food for our journey together with Him and with one another. That as we gather around that table, it becomes for us the very meeting place of earth and heaven, the connection between the material and the spiritual, the visible and the invisible, the all too human and the divine.

If then I was to plump for one or the other, it would have to be a table, albeit that it is an altar at which Jesus' sacrifice is represented, that we might be remembered as one body. A table because it was Jesus' practice on Earth to sit and eat with sinners. It was at a table that He was revealed to those two disciples and it was in their home, at an ordinary table. For when we gather we sit around a table, rather than gaze upwards to a high altar at which the priest alone stands. For all are welcome, saints and sinners all, equally known and equally graced nonetheless by him who knows us and loves us, despite ourselves and our ongoing propensity to mess up.

We gather around that table all equally addicted to our egos, our need for security, our unwillingness to relinquish the game of comparison and making ourselves feel better at the expense of others. We gather around that table and kneel in supplication that we be re-encountered by Him who meets us there in our need and into whose hands He places himself, as broken bread and wine, outpoured that we might be and do the same. That as we return to our seats and from there are sent on our way back to our everyday lives, we will be willing once again to be broken , to be *seen* as broken, to be vulnerable and to be willing to be outpoured for the sake of others and for this world that God so loves.

A table then, because that is the place of hospitality, that sacred ancient duty that we only gradually discovered here at St Paul's was indeed the place for encounter, for lives to touch, for stories to be told and so for Jesus to be encountered in our midst. A table because every time we eat we say grace, we express our gratitude to our heavenly Father for his provision, not only for ourselves, but for all his children. And so a table to which *all* are invited, *all* are welcome and to which we cannot come without an awareness of the needs of others in our community and across the world; for those whose needs *have* been provided, but because of human greed, in which we are implicated, they cannot share in them.

And a visual aid not just of our inter-connectedness with Jesus our companion, the bread of life with us, or with our brothers and sisters across the world, but also with the very creation itself, for it is the fruit thereof that we eat. We are all interdependent within the community that is creation and that too we dare not ever forget. A table too because it is here that the Lord comes, it is here that that ancient cry "Maranatha, come Lord Jesus", is fulfilled as we gather, eat and drink, week by week by week.

So finally we shall come in **chapter 5** to the Lord's Prayer that Jesus taught and which we and that early Church take as our model. We will debunk the mechanistic view of prayer that so many then and still believe is how prayer is to be understood. And having dispensed with the idea that if we fulfil the conditions perfectly, God will answer our prayers, we will turn ourselves to Jesus' own personal experience in prayer. Simply the fact of his prayer life would be model and encouragement enough for us to continue to pray.

But that his experience of prayer, which punctuated his public ministry, was bracketed by his experience in the wilderness and then finally in the Garden of Gethsemane, will teach us a huge amount about our legitimate expectation in turning to prayer. Jesus' teaching of the Lord's Prayer is placed, by Luke at least, in the context of a story Jesus tells about a friend enabling his friend to provide hospitality at midnight to an unexpected guest who had arrived after everyone has gone to bed.

The answer is ultimately forthcoming, but not in response to legitimate and reasonable requests or even for the shame that that friend might have experienced had he not been able to provide such hospitality, but rather, altogether and entirely at the householder's discretion. Jesus concludes that the Father will answer our prayers not specifically, as we might have hoped, but in the person of the Holy Spirit, who will be with us and enable us to bear whatever may befall, just as Jesus did when he cried out in agony that he might not have to drink the cup, but knowing that he would have to drink it to the full. He simply trusted His heavenly Father, that underneath were the everlasting arms, even though his experience in that moment was one of despair and forsakenness.

Jesus' teaching on prayer, therefore, is rooted in His own experience and must, because he was THE man, be universally applicable. Whatever it is that prayer may be, the idea that God might answer my prayer, for example for a parking space, whilst at the same time be deaf to the prayers of millions of my brothers and sisters for enough to eat today, is simply absurd, even distasteful and makes God out to be heartless, even a caricature. It may go a long way towards explaining why so many in the West find such a self-absorbed brand of Christianity so distasteful. Almost every word therefore in Jesus' model prayer, which we now refer to as the Lord's Prayer, is of significance and worthy of our close attention.

And perhaps the opening words sum up just how significant and radical was Jesus' view of prayer then and I would say still is. For in three simple words, Jesus collectivises prayer, universalises the human condition and recasts God as a prodigal Father and then with the fourth, brings the reality of heaven into the midst of our earthly condition. From this perspective, this starting point, all else flows. God is not just 'my' but 'our' Heavenly Father, we are all God's children and whatever is good for one child must be good for another. We are all therefore, it turns out, our brother's and our sister's keepers.

The prayer is a request, first and foremost, that that heavenly reality, that divine will that all His children live in peace, (Shalom, Abuntu), might always and everywhere be becoming an earthly reality. That what Jesus the great High Priest has accomplished once and for all upon the Cross, might be the source of blessing to all God's children and not just the chosen, self-selecting few!

That the reality of Jesus' self-sacrificial life of service to and of others, might become the way to life here and now on earth, for one and all. That all might eat the bread of heaven, the food of justice and peace and of actual as well as the sacramental bread of life. That 'Jubilee', the release from debt, might not simply be a wonderful idea, but the reality in and out of which all nations might live towards one another, as well as in our personal lives towards our brothers and sisters.

That our blindness to the comparative, judgemental blame games that we all play, to give ourselves an ephemeral and illusory sense of self over and against others, might be brought out into the light as we gradually and collectively learn not to go down that path, but rather join a twelve-step programme, one model of church we have explored, and be authentic, vulnerable and courageous in our endeavours to play a new game of love, service and forgiveness towards others.

That in so doing, we might find ourselves together delivered from the lies and deceit that the evil one has so well convinced us of, individually and internationally, that the way to everlasting peace is through violence and bloodshed, when Jesus proclaimed once and for all, that that way is "finished". It was never God's way, it was always the means to which men resorted, structuring the world to the advantage of the few and the detriment of the vast majority of God's children.

In these five chapters then, we will trace the early Church's' experience of refashioning humanity in the image of Jesus, THE archetypal human being who, in fulfilling God's covenant with his ancient people in their promised land, universalised that covenant to include all peoples of whatever estate or condition, extended to the entire world. Jesus was not founding a new religion, but recalling humanity to its true calling and its true sense of self.

This book is written in the conviction that if the Church were to model itself once more upon Jesus, rather than on its sense of itself as being an institution, with all its buildings and its bureaucracy, and if it could repent of its history, that has not only lost contact with its captain, pioneer and model, but has also been so guilty of abuse and of false testimony, and reprioritise itself around the things outlined in these five chapters, then it would have a huge impact in the twenty-first century. If it does not do this, it will continue to drift into the oblivion of the widespread disinterest that it currently experiences in the West and so richly deserves for its failings.

Chapter 1

They devoted themselves...
Then some of the believers who belonged to the party of
the Pharisees... (Acts 15:5)

Immediately after Peter's sermon on that first Pentecost, recorded for us in the second chapter of the book of Acts, we read these words:

"They devoted themselves to the Apostle's teaching and to the fellowship, to the breaking of bread and to prayer." (Acts 2:42)

In this book, I want to explore four aspects of this verse which I believe are necessary and constitutive of what it means to be 'in Christ' (Christian), a member of the body of Christ, and of what it means to be one of those who, in this early record of the church's history, were known as followers of 'the way'.

It seems to me that the words of this verse are particularly significant and pertinent for the universal church at the beginning of another millennium and in the light of its less than favourable history – the abuse of power, persecution, resistance to change and cover-up – for surely, these words can enable the Church to reorient itself in their light.

Before we can attend to what it was that was the object of 'their' devotion however, we need to ask: who were these people who 'devoted themselves'? To answer this we need to recognise that in the book of Acts we are given a parallel presentation of the missions of Peter and of Paul. We need also to recognise that these missions were, at times, divergent and that there was considerable conflict between them. The Apostle Paul, Apostle to the Gentiles, preaching a Gospel of freedom and liberty, was in direct opposition to Peter, who preached a more conservative Gospel with its emphasis on the centrality of Jerusalem, the priesthood and a zeal for the law.

In his letter to the Corinthians at the beginning of his apostolic life and his letter to the Romans written towards the end of his life, Paul contrasts the attitudes and actions of the weak and the strong in this nascent faith. Those who styled themselves as 'strong' he regards as 'weak', thus reversing their labels, whilst those labelled 'weak', by the self-styled strong, he regards as strong (Rom.14/1 Cor.8).

Those concerned then about prescriptions and restrictions, special days, circumcision, foods that should or should not be eaten, as well as what was and was not permissible on the Sabbath, would in our day be those who might describe themselves as 'conservative' or 'traditionalists', and resistant, for example, to the ordination of women. According to the Apostle Paul, they, are 'weak' in the faith, and worthy of special sensitivity, therefore, by those to whom he was writing, who were unconcerned with such traditions and prescription, and who in our day might be labelled as 'liberal', but whom Paul regarded as 'strong' in the faith.

It is therefore somewhat ironic that this same Apostle has in our day become associated with a more conservative, limiting, restrictive interpretation of the faith, when in his own day, he was regarded as a radical heretic, and the one who threatened the ancient and traditional interpretation of their Scriptures. So, in his letter to the Galatians, when he is possibly at his most argumentative, Paul makes this explosive contrast. His more restrictive, traditional Jewish brethren (with whom Peter has associated himself), he calls the descendants of Hagar the slave-woman, with whom Abraham conceived a child, whilst the true descendants and heirs of the Covenant promise made to Sarah and Abraham were the Gentiles, who have been delivered from the burdensome yoke and prescriptions of the law. As he declares: "It is for freedom that Christ has set you free!"

In the book of Acts, we read of the relationship between those first male Jews who had journeyed to Jerusalem to celebrate the feast of Pentecost, having responded to Peter's sermon that day in the Temple. We also hear about the Gentile Roman Centurion, who invites Peter to his house and who also experiences the convicting and assuring work of the Holy Spirit, as well as the Gentile Ethiopian Eunuch, who, though barred from Temple worship, nevertheless had journeyed to Jerusalem to worship and who experienced the assurance of the Holy Spirit that he too is a child of God. This is the extremely sensitive material of historical record, which remains to this day political and religious dynamite.

Lines were drawn then and there between the more liberal interpretation of the new things that God had done in Jesus Christ, with its greater freedom regarding the law and for example the status of women, represented by Paul. For according to Paul, not only was there a reversal of the historic interpretation as regards Jew and Gentile, slave and free, but also as regards men and women. According to Paul, all were equal, equally free, one in Christ Jesus and without status distinction within the body of Christ.

Thus Paul can quite easily and freely as well as provocatively include Junia, a woman in the apostolic group (Rom.16:7) and it is certainly worthy of note that until relatively recently, she was unsurprisingly given the male name Junias by male translators!

The more Jewish and traditional interpretation, with a greater regard for the law, Temple ritual and patriarchy, was represented by Peter and James. The one with a vision of all those in Christ being *new creations and temples* of the Holy Spirit, the other with Jewish priorities centred on the re-establishment of a purified Temple in Jerusalem. The one Gentile, centred upon the missionary work, preaching and teaching of Paul, the Apostle to the Gentiles, the other Jewish, represented by Peter and James, who became the elders and primary pillars of the Jewish believers in Jerusalem and with influence amongst Jews dispersed around the Roman Empire.

The Apostles of both 'sides' anticipated the imminent return of Christ, but both would be disappointed, because just as His people had rejected him during His incarnation, the majority in Israel still refused to recognise Jesus as Yahweh, the Lord of their Scriptures and would further reject the Apostolic plea to turn to their Christ. This would inevitably lead to a need for each branch of what would become the new religion called 'Christianity' to reinterpret its understanding of the revelation that their Apostles had received from the risen Jesus Christ.

Especially so after the destruction of Jerusalem in AD 70, which heralded the end of the sacrificial system as well as the priesthood, and as the tenth Jubilee ended, sounded the death knell to the hopes for this nascent sect which would become 'Christianity' of Jesus' return, as well as those of the Jewish people for the coming of their Christ. The focus for the Jewish people and their religion, which we know today as Judaism, would be their Scriptures alone.

For this nascent sect, which had struggled, through Peter and James to remain faithful to its parent religion, challenged as they were by Paul's radical opening up of the promise to their forefathers by the inclusion of the Gentiles, it would mean a final and irrevocable split from Judaism, a split which has tragically echoed down the centuries. For nascent 'Christianity' split within itself right from the start, and the focus for these Jewish believers would become the coming of Christ through the Eucharist and the breaking of bread, as expressed by John in his Gospel, whilst for the Gentile followers of Jesus, their focus became their fellowship as the Church (which they understood to be Christ's body here on Earth) to whom and through whom He 'came'. This is something we will return to in a later chapter.

Both sets of believers placed their emphasis upon their Apostle's teaching, yet expressed it in different ways, which lead to conflict between them. They had different attitudes towards the fellowship, collective meals, the celebration of the Eucharist, and the Law. For the conservative Jewish contingent, such laws, rules and actions were the very definition of righteousness, in contrast to those Gentile followers of Paul, who had far more liberal attitudes and for whom Jesus' summary of the Law and the 'rule' of love would be central.

For the conservative branch, warnings concerning the dire consequences of falling short, (which were entirely in keeping with the thundering of Ancient Israel's prophets) would be how their Apostles expressed themselves towards those who sought to walk in the way, whilst for Gentile followers of Jesus, who listened to and heard the letters of their Apostle Paul, it would be his assurances that nothing could separate them from the love of God in Christ Jesus, that would give them security in their journey of faith. These are two very different ways to write and hear Scripture which we need to be aware of.

The New Testament itself bears witness to the disagreement between these two groupings and the divergent ways in which they read what they regarded as Scripture at that time, namely the Hebrew Scriptures, in at least three ways.

First, there is the narrative record of the book of Acts, which resulted in a compromise arrangement between the two groups, concerning what was felt to be appropriate table fellowship at the Jerusalem Council, outlined in Acts chapter 15. This issue may seem trifling to us, but it was rooted in the way each group regarded the authority of the Law.

The second was the massive disagreement between the Apostles Paul and Peter, alluded to in Paul's letter to the Galatians. Once again the issue is table fellowship, Peter having withdrawn from accompanying Gentile Christians when they ate, once a group of conservative law-abiding Jewish Christians arrived from Jerusalem. Paul does not spare Peter's blushes, regarding his action as anti-Gospel and "anathema".

The third way in which the New Testament bears eloquent witness to this divide is in its very structure. For there are nine letters to the Gentile churches, mostly regarded to have been from the hand of the Apostle Paul (that is, Romans to Thessalonians) and there are nine letters or pieces of writing, (from Hebrews to Revelation) which are obviously more Jewish in content and directed towards Jewish believers.

For Paul, THE sacrament of the alternative Empire of Jesus is the church, the body of Christ on Earth and it is *to* the churches and *of* the church that he writes. This fellowship, to whom he writes, is an inclusive egalitarian mix of people who are no longer in the flesh solely, but are now indwelt by the Holy spirit, temples of the Holy Spirit, no less, over whom the yoke of Moses has no power. And whilst there may have been a season of disobedience for the Gentiles, now, as a result of Israel's unwillingness to receive their Christ, the Gentiles have been brought into the Abrahamic covenant as promised.

God chose to work through Abram (meaning simply 'father'), whose name was changed to Abraham (the Father of the Nations) and the Apostle Paul now sees this fulfilled in the person of Christ, as a blessing to all peoples, with the further result that the anticipated Parousia or return of Christ, so evident in his earliest letters to the church in Thessalonica, has morphed into an anticipation of the presence of Christ in and through the fellowship which is Christ's body on Earth.

The nine pieces of writing directed towards those who are Jewish, on the other hand, and in which there is virtually no mention of the church, are variously introduced thus: "To the Hebrews" (earliest manuscripts) (Heb. 1:1) "To the twelve tribes scattered among the nations" (James 1:1) "To God's elect" (1 Peter 1:1/2, 2 Peter 3:1) "You are a chosen people, a royal priesthood, a holy nation, a people belonging to God" (1 Peter 2:9). Indeed it is not entirely clear whether these are written exclusively to Jewish Christians or simply to Jews living away from Jerusalem.

In these we find special reference to the Temple, the re-establishment of God's reign on Earth centred in Jerusalem, the ingathering of the righteous remnant of God's elect people, Ancient Israel, hence the emphasis upon the Law of Moses and the establishment of God's reign on Earth through this royal priestly line in the order of Melchizedek, who is both High Priest and sacrifice.

The Apostle John reveals in the book of Revelation that this establishment of God's reign will be through the New Jerusalem descending from heaven and not through the re-establishment of an earthly Jerusalem, with the destruction of which, these Jews finally have to accept that the presence of the Lord will be experienced with his people through the Eucharist. This seems to be the primary purpose of the Gospel of John.

In his sermon on that Pentecost Sunday, Peter claims that it was to Jesus that ancient Israel's King David spoke when he called him Lord, that is, 'Yahweh' of their Hebrew Scriptures, the promised Christ, the Holy one and that the King that David was promised would sit on his throne forever (Acts 2:25-31). Three thousand men responded positively to Peter's words that day, but the vast majority did not. To those who did not respond with warmth, Peter's words were anathema.

Thus, the Hebrew 'Christians' were not only at odds with their Hebrew brethren in Jerusalem and throughout the Roman Empire, but also with their Gentile brethren, who had become followers in the way, as Luke termed them in his written record, penned much later of course. It is important that we bear in mind that only later would they be referred to as 'Christians', a term of abuse used against them, and especially so by Jews, who were gradually distancing themselves from this nascent sect within their midst.

As a result, the Hebrew 'Christians' sought to reassure their law-abiding and Temple-attending Jewish brethren, (centred in Jerusalem as were they), who remained unconvinced of the merits of this so called 'Christ', of their allegiance to all things associated with their religion. This meant walking the tightrope of disassociation with their fellow Gentile followers in the way – a difficult line for them to walk and conflict was inevitable.

Now this may all have seemed a somewhat unnecessary digression, but I believe it to have been important for a number of reasons. First, for some readers, every word of the Bible is to be viewed as the absolute, literal, inerrant, and equally authoritative word of God. For such readers, the idea that God's self-revelation might have been adaptive to the culture and times in which it was revealed and that it might even be wrong or that different portions contradict each other, is impossible to accept. But even the limited evidence of the different interpretations and value placed on particular portions of the Hebrew Scriptures, and in particular the Law, as well as the obvious disagreement between two Apostles, who would then go on to contribute portions from their very different (opposing) perspectives, to what we now call the New Testament, seems to me to make this abundantly clear.

Furthermore, the idea that Jesus might abrogate some, if not much of what we read in the Hebrew Scriptures, is likewise anathema to some, but this is precisely what we shall discover when we turn to the chapter on the Apostle's teaching. For Jesus rereads those Hebrew Scriptures and requires us to do the same. That was difficult for Peter's audience on the day of Pentecost and continues to be difficult to this day. The God who progressively reveals himself to ancient Israel, accommodates himself to their needs and their circumstances time and time again, whether that be in terms of meat eating, polygamy, city building, King making or a number of laws concerning the treatment of slaves, to give but a few examples.

Now whilst this may seem difficult enough to some readers, the idea that that progression continues through the New Testament is even more challenging. As we have seen, the early Church, as well as the Messianic sect within the Judaism of the day, had to come to terms over a period of 40 years, from Jesus' death to the destruction of Jerusalem and the Temple, (a time during which much of what we now read as the New Testament was written), with the reality that the expected return of their Christ was being indefinitely delayed and this, in the face of the direct revelation of Jesus himself to both groups, namely the Apostle Paul, the beneficiary of direct revelation (Gal. 1:12), who states that Christ will return soon (1Thess. 4:15-18) and the Apostle John, who by direct revelation (Rev. 1:1) confirms that Jesus is coming soon (Rev. 22:7).

Both Apostles apparently simply got this revelation wrong. Jesus did not come back soon or in their lifetimes. We have to acknowledge this and think about what our view of authority of the Bible is and how it is to be understood, or bury our heads in the sand and pretend either that it isn't there or that we do not read 'a canon within a canon' i.e. selectively, which of course we all do and with good warrant, for as we shall see, that is precisely what Jesus did! Some parts of Scripture are clearly far more important than others.

God's self-revelation is cumulative, progressive and does conflict. We cannot and must not hold our rational capacities to ransom to the inerrancy of every word of the Bible. And furthermore, we must also recognise that what has seemed to be the meaning of the authoritative word of Scripture throughout most of the church's history has, it turns out, also been wrong. An example of this is the way in which slavery was regarded until the nineteenth century, as having been instituted by God and supported by the authority of the Bible.

That interpretation was obviously wrong by modern standards. And I could develop other more controversial interpretative conflicts which seem to me to exist, but there is no need here, for surely the point is made: we need to appreciate that words or texts in the Bible cannot simply be lifted off the page and applied with authority, without that being confirmed by the Spirit within us, as well as by our own experience and the wisdom of others, who over the years have also sought to interpret its meaning.

Last, we need to recognise that the Bible was often born out of conflict; that those who seek to interpret it will often be at odds with one another and that that is not the end of the world for the Church, as we shall see in our chapter on 'The Fellowship'. If two great Apostles could be so at odds with one another, then it is more than likely that we shall be so also. But that does not mean that one wing is right and the other wrong, but rather that one wing is temperamentally conservative and the other temperamentally liberal and it would be nice to think that we would attempt to agree to disagree, amicably, rather than fall out so drastically, like Peter and Paul.

All that said, and with it in our minds, we can now turn to consider the role of the Messianic sect within Judaism, or the churches of Gentiles, as sacraments of the alternative Empire that Jesus proclaimed and incarnated. For the rest of this book and for the sake of ease, I will refer to this two-branch, nascent religion, at odds with both the religion that birthed it and the Empire within which it gradually established itself, as 'the church'. And that church is neither the alternative Empire itself, nor capable of being manifested in any form that is constituted by violence, oppression or injustice, whether that be the Empire of Rome or any other less obvious form it may take in our day and age, despite the fact that this is precisely what we have witnessed in church history, not only in the Holy Roman Empire, with state and church wedded as one, but also in the form of several Protestant States after the Reformation. I believe the Church and the state can never be one, for they are two separate if related institutions created by God with different purposes.

It was no surprise that one of the charges against Jesus at his mock trial was that of insurrection, for Jesus proclaimed an alternative heavenly Kingdom. At the same time, Jesus remained, as did the early Church, a part of the religion of his day, a faithful attendee at the feasts in the Temple in Jerusalem, as well as at his local synagogue, at least at the beginning of his ministry, when he caused such a stir.

Whilst the Empire of Heaven that would be incarnated on Earth would extend to the four corners of the known world, like its earthly counterpart in Rome, neither its methodology, nor its force, nor its government (which included the equal participation of all, giving special priority to those who were viewed within the Roman Empire, as well as within the religion of Judaism, as untouchable – the least, the last and the lost) would, should or could, ever reflect any earthly Empire.

Moreover, although this Heavenly Empire was coextensive with that of Rome, it was manifest in a mysterious, upside down, 'the first shall be last' kind of way. Its methodology would be the death of the ego, combined with the love of neighbour, including an enemy, rather than the death of that enemy. It would be manifest as its members broke the cycle of suspicion and mistreatment of others and attempted to incarnate Jesus' teaching about treating others as we would want to be treated ourselves. This was as radical then as it remains today.

In practice of course, this was never going to be a mass populist movement. There are too many people, not to mention powers, who are invested in the status quo, a status quo which benefits the few to the detriment of the many. The church will only ever be a small unimpressive, messy, mixed up community that will have particular appeal to those on the margins of polite society, as Jesus proclaimed almost with his first public statement: "Blessed are the poor, for theirs is the Empire of Heaven." and that will offer little appeal to those to whom Jesus would say, "Woe to you who are rich….".

What then did it mean for those early 'Christians' to be part of the church? What was the relationship between the establishment of the Empire of Heaven and the church? What was the relationship of those first Jewish Christians, a sect within their own religion, to that religion? How did they view themselves vis-a-vis their Gentile counterparts? How were they viewed and how did they view themselves vis-a- vis their fellow Jews and their own Scriptures (that is, what we now call the Old Testament)? And in the light of the answers to those questions, what then does it mean *for us* to be members of this rag tag gathering of people, called *church?*

If becoming a Holy Roman Empire turned out to be a false trail, how was it that Christianity became a religion in its own right in the first place, rather than simply being a sect within the Judaism of its day? Or rather, what was it that ultimately forced or required such a split? For even to talk in terms of the early 'church' is to recognise that the first 'Christians' wanted to express their sense of their faith's continuity with the Judaism that birthed it. For the term 'ecclesia' from which is derived our word 'church', was one of the two words in their Scriptures that described the fathered people of God, the other being 'sunagos' which they could not choose for obvious reasons, namely that it was the name given to gatherings of those who would become known as 'Jews'.

I think it would be fair to say that the early dispute which sounded the death knell for this new vibrant sect remaining within Judaism, was not in the first instance the claim that Jesus had risen from the dead, and not even necessarily Jesus' radical teaching, but rather it was that these first Jewish 'Christians' immediately worshipped Jesus (a man) as the LORD, THE manifestation of God on earth, Yahweh of the Hebrew Scriptures.

This proved intolerable to the majority opinion within the Judaism of the day, even though the possibility of God being manifest in person and appearing on earth to people, was a self-evident fact of their Scriptures. Nonetheless, it was this which was disputed then and which remains divisive to this day. The Judaism that we recognise today is entirely monotheistic, but according to the minority view within the Judaism of Jesus' day, (and later the normative and orthodox view within 'Christianity'), it was most certainly not.

This change occurred fairly rapidly as a result of the persecution that broke out which produced the split. On the one hand, the God whom all Jews worshipped was "one" and on the other hand, this one God had been revealed throughout ancient Israel's history to patriarchs, judges, priests, kings and prophets, as Creator and Redeemer and as both power and wisdom and who also, in the person of Yahweh, the "LORD", was the human incarnation of God most High. This of course is far more recognisable to those who are 'Christian' as the relationship between God as Father and God as Son.

As Jesus himself would say, "No one has seen the Father except the Son" (Matt. 11:27), and "I and the Father are one" (John 17:11). Therefore, immediately after his resurrection, the realisation that the Yahweh of their Scriptures translated into Greek as LORD, meant that rather than merely following him as their teacher, they worshipped him as the Lord, as the manifestation, in person, of God most High.

To what became the majority view within Judaism, this was of course anathema. Strangely, it seems also to have become the view accepted by Christian interpreters of the Old Testament today. Presumably this has something to do with an insecurity about being viewed as anti-Semitic if they read their Scriptures in a non-monotheistic way, which is precisely what I am suggesting the first Christians did and which caused their persecution by the Jews of their day and then the split between what became the two religions.

41

So let me highlight a few verses to show how those early 'Christians' managed to prove from their Scriptures that which confirmed their experience of the man Jesus, whom they witnessed in person both before and after his resurrection as their Lord, Yahweh. There are two texts that Paul quotes which are generally regarded as very early. The first is a hymn, to which Paul alludes and from which he quotes words originally attributed to Yahweh, the Lord, the anointed Christ, the Servant of God most High:

"Christ Jesus who being in very nature God became a servant (Isaiah 52:13), a lamb to the slaughter (Isaiah 53:7), obedient unto death, so that at the Name of Jesus every knee shall bow and every tongue confess that Jesus is the Christ, the LORD, to the glory of God the Father" (Isaiah 45:23), (Phil. 2:6-1). In the second, Paul quotes the affirmation that Jesus is both Israel's Christ and her Lord, "declared to be Son of God by virtue of his resurrection from the dead", (Rom.1:3/4).

In like manner, for on this both Apostles to Jews and Gentiles could agree, the Apostle John, can say that Jesus is the Logos, "the Word, who was with God in the beginning and is God himself", (John 1:1) once again two, yet also one. He says that although, as the majority view amongst the Jews of the day and also the contemporary view says, God could not be seen, one thread within their Scriptures attests to the fact that He has now been made known in this Jesus, as the "Word became flesh and dwelt amongst them", (John 1:18) and they beheld his Glory, "the Glory of the One and Only", (John 1:14). As the rest of his Gospel would attempt to demonstrate, this Jesus, is both the Word and God, Lord and

Christ, the Incarnation of the most High, the Son of his Father, two yet one.

One like a Son of Man (Jesus' self-designation), is presented to the antecedent of time and enthroned with him, as recorded in Daniel chapter 7 and as replicated in the Book of Revelation, with the slain lamb sharing the throne with the Lord God Almighty: "To him who sits on the throne and to the lamb be praise and honour and glory and power for ever and ever", (Rev. 5: 13). And a repetition of this in a different form by the Apostle to the Gentiles says: "There is but one God, the Father from whom all things came and for whom we live, AND there is but one Lord, Jesus Christ, through whom all things came and through whom we live". (1Cor. 8:6). Two, yet one.

The theophanies of Yahweh found in the Hebrew Scriptures are finally and fully manifest in the Incarnation of Jesus. Texts about Yahweh are simply assumed to be applicable to Jesus: "Blessed is the person against whom the Lord will not reckon his sin." (Psalm 32:2/Rom. 4:8). "Everyone who calls on the name of the Lord will be saved." (Joel 2:32/Rom. 10:13). "The rock", a title usually reserved for Yahweh in Deuteronomy is attributed to Jesus (Deut. 32:4/18/31) who is also the one who led them out of Egypt (1Cor. 10: 1-11). According to both Peter and Paul, He is their Saviour, another function specifically reserved for Yahweh in the Hebrew Scriptures, whilst the 'I AM' sayings of John's Gospel are especially decisive in this regard and shocking as much now as then, for those who heard them "drew back and fell to the ground."(John 18:6).

Jesus' prayer at the last supper, recorded in that same Gospel, clearly articulates his sense of his divine son-ship, his relationship to His Heavenly Father, in such a way that it is clear that there are and have always been two, the unseen God most High and the visible manifestation of God in the person of his Son, Yahweh, the Lord, distinct, yet also one. This is echoed by Paul in his benedictions: "May our God and Father himself, *and* our Lord Jesus Christ direct our way." (1 Thess. 3:11/12 et al) and which the Apostles to the Jews, Peter and John take up in their doxologies in the worship of Jesus as Lord (2 Peter 3:18/Rev. 1:5/6).

These early Christians believed themselves to be those who had realised that Jesus was the fulfilment of their Scriptures. They believed that Yahweh, the LORD, who had promised through his prophets that he, the Holy One of the most high God, would come in the person of the anointed one, the Christ of God, the suffering servant, a High Priest, in the order of Melchizedek, (rather than by descent through the brother of Moses, that is, Aaron) had now come in the person of Jesus.

At first the early Christians tried to remain within the Judaism of their day, hence Peter's sermon given in the Temple precincts in Jerusalem that first Pentecost. But as it became clearer how their interpretation of their Scriptures was so divergent, it became impossible for this to be sustained. The persecution of the first Christians by the Jews and within a generation, the destruction of the Temple in Jerusalem, meant that Judaism would become the people of the Hebrew Scriptures alone awaiting the Christ who would restore their now destroyed Temple in Jerusalem. (In passing it is worth noting that a similarly 'Apocalyptic' view is held by fundamentalist Christians and explains the passion with

44

which Jewish Zionists and such Christian Zionists view Jerusalem).

Early Christians took a rather different path, which as we have already seen, was also split into two. On the one hand they viewed Jesus as the High Priest, their leaders as His priests on earth and his presence manifest in the Eucharist. On the other hand, they viewed one another as temples of the Holy Spirit, his presence manifest in their collectivism as Christ's body on Earth, with Christ as the head, their true worship being their daily lives poured out in self-sacrificial love.

Thus, in response to these very divergent interpretations of their inherited Scripture, which we now call the Old Testament, and in the light of their experience of Jesus, whom they all regarded as the manifestation of Yahweh, the LORD, these two wings developed semi-independently within the Roman Empire, wherein Caesar was worshipped as the LORD! One branch was more conservative, and early on remained a part of an accepted religion within the Empire, whilst the other more liberal Gentile branch was always a minority sect within a Judaism that persecuted it, and despised by fellow Jewish followers in the way, it would remain unrecognised by the Roman Empire and periodically persecuted by that Empire also.

One branch was particular about conditions of membership, prioritising those who were Jews on the basis of their election as God's chosen people and holding to the view that in order to become a Messianic Jew, Gentiles needed both to embrace the Law of Moses and be circumcised as the sign of God's covenant with their forefather Abram. The other branch modelled itself on Jesus' practice and bias toward the poor, the welcoming of the least, the last and the lost, and on the sacred duty of hospitality, now crucially extended to all. Jesus' willingness to eat with 'sinners' showed that they too were members of God's covenant with Abraham, the Father of all Nations.

One branch regarded itself as a faithful remnant, (*the sunagos of God*) who worshipped in the Temple in Jerusalem, the other as the new ecclesia of God, in continuity with, yet the fulfilment of, God's calling of all peoples. The one prioritised the Law, the ingathering of all peoples to Jerusalem and gradually, as hope faded for His return, the coming of Christ in the Eucharist; the other, the coming of Christ when two or three gathered, as the new fellowship in the light of their Apostle's teaching about the Gospel of freedom from the Law of Moses, and the equality of all in Christ. Though expressed in different ways, these two branches of faith kept central their conviction of the authority of their shared Scriptures and on the fulfilment of God's purposes through the atoning sacrifice of Christ, fostering an understanding that Christ himself was the rebuilt Temple.

The two pillars of Scripture and Eucharist, became foundational for the early Church, representing the two major strands of ancient Israel's history and the revelation of God in the person of Yahweh as Creator and Redeemer, all this evidenced by the verse which is the subject of this book.

Tragically, these two branches, the one more conservative in its interpretation of Scripture and the other more liberal, the one somewhat more exclusive and the other aspiring to be more inclusive, rather than being mutually supporting pillars in the structure of the church, have remained the two rival wings to this day. How sad that the split between those first

Christians and the faith that birthed them, is replicated within the Church to this day. How sad that these two wings, rather than complementing one another and being of equal emphasis, as they were in that first church, should be at such odds with one another.

The ending of Luke's Gospel is significant in this regard and illustrates it well, for as the two disciples remembered what Jesus had said to them, their "hearts burned within them" as they sat at table and ate with Him and it was as He "broke the bread" that they recognised him (Luke 24). The inclusive table fellowship of Jesus, the breaking of bread, the giving of thanks in prayer and the authority of their scriptures being deliberately highlighted. It therefore being no surprise that it is these elements which are highlighted once again by Luke as being the focus of the early church and the subject of this book.

Moreover, as the early Church's hopes of Jesus coming back to Earth from Heaven receded, they had to further reinterpret those Scriptures and their understanding of them and begin to appreciate that when they prayed, "Thy Kingdom come", and when they cried, "Maranatha, come Lord, come!", that Jesus, Yahweh, the LORD, would come to them as they participated in the Eucharist, as they prayed, as they were the body of Christ to one another, as they were that broken body for the life of the world and as they were fed by those same Scriptures; indeed, as they devoted themselves to these four cornerstones of the faith, to which we shall shortly turn.

The inclusion of the Gentiles into God's covenant with Abraham, born out of their experience of the Spirit of God in their midst, had two implications: the Holy Spirit was no longer the property of ancient Israel, nor was he/she the property of God's new ecclesia, for that same Holy Spirit had now been poured out on all peoples (to which that first Pentecost sermon bore witness).

Jesus, as THE incarnation of Yahweh the Lord, was the one in and through and for whom all things in all creation hold together (Col. 1), and not only the creator but also the sustainer of the entire creation. As the Lord, Yahweh, he was *the* image bearer, par excellence, of God most high, the restorer of that which the first Adam lost: "As in Adam all die so in Christ shall all be made alive" (1Cor. 15:22).

Or, as one of the Apostles to the Jewish believers would say, Jesus "is the beginning and the end" (Rev. 1), "the light and life of all peoples" (John 1) and who records Jesus himself as saying, "When I am lifted up I will draw all peoples to myself" (John 13:32). The truth which both wings of this nascent fellowship came to understand and could agree on was that the Gospel was the good news of what God had now accomplished in and through Jesus, the LORD, Yahweh, for everyone, however much they may have argued about table etiquette!

So it meant that in principle none could be excluded, for Peter's vision recorded later in chapter 10 of the book of Acts confirms that nothing and no one in all creation can now be regarded as unclean. The conversion of the Ethiopian Eunuch, recorded earlier in Acts chapter 8, should have functioned as a huge banner or signpost for the emerging Jewish church concerning who is accepted into the church and who is not. Their Jewish Scriptures made it perfectly clear that such a person could never enter the Temple and yet here was the Spirit directly countermanding those very Scriptures, fulfilling them in a way that was as unanticipated as it was unacceptable, just as we shall see Jesus himself did.

For Jesus began his ministry by putting in opposition His own words with His own people's Scriptures, "You have heard...but I tell you" and yet could assert that he had not come to abolish those very Scriptures but to fulfil them! (Matt. 5). Thus the ecclesia, unlike the sunagos, birthed as it was in Jesus' inclusive table fellowship, was called so that God's people on Earth could be to be a "light to the nations". God's people could no longer be contained within the religion of Judaism or a narrow strip of land, for the Gospel was for all peoples and indeed for all creation.

It was an ecclesia like the renewed Jerusalem which is coming down from heaven, whose gates are permanently open and to which the nations are bringing all their human accomplishments. This is the calling of the Church down the centuries. God's 'open door' policy is not an easy one, but we should not be surprised by this, for the history of the early Church's conflict, not to mention the slowness of Jesus' disciples to grasp the breadth and length and height and depth of God who is Love, for all his children, regardless, bears eloquent testimony to the difficulty of that challenge.

The theology of the ecclesia must therefore attempt to incarnate Jesus' welcoming of sinners, prostitutes and publicans; it must attempt to replicate Jesus' communication of outward purity, rather than fear of being tainted by those who do not fulfil some kind of entry requirement or condition. It is one of the reasons why the liturgy we use at infant baptism is so significant when it states that Jesus came into the world, lived, taught, died, rose and ascended to the right hand side of the Father, as an expression of God's love for this child, even though the child has no clue yet, that this is the case.

This is not to say, however, that the 'law' of love is any less demanding than the Law of Moses and yet according to Jesus, its burden is nonetheless light. The Apostle Paul and his Gospel were criticised for being light on works and obedience and heavy on freedom and grace. So the challenge for both wings of the inheritors of the two threads of apostolic teaching remain, the one to be inclusive, the other to witness to their freedom in Christ through love of their neighbour.

There will be, of course, those who exclude themselves, indeed the majority of this country who are not present when the ecclesia gathers, but please, please, let it no longer be because that ecclesia is either an exclusive, irrelevant, boring, self-righteous, religious, narrow-minded judgemental club or because that ecclesia is so permissive and so accepting that it is indistinguishable from those in the midst of whom it exists. This is no easy path, it was not then and it is not now.

The first followers of Jesus agreed that He was the Christ, the incarnation of Yahweh the Lord, which brought them into conflict with both the established orthodoxy within the Judaism of their day, as well as with the Empire for whom Caesar was Lord. Their internal table fellowship disagreements added further fuel to the fire of conflict between those who were more conservative and those who were more liberal.

But a theology of ecclesia, born as it was out of a divided Judaism, and ultimately cast out as it was, for its radical re-interpretation of the Hebrew Scriptures in the light of Jesus' example and teaching, when it insists that all peoples, and especially those on the margins, are equally God's children, in whom the light and life of Christ is inextinguishable, is as challenging now as ever it was then.

And here is the thing: whether those who are not a part of that ecclesia acknowledge that light, life and love or not, it remains true. I am not suggesting that this is easy, but it seems to me that the ecclesia, if it is to be true to its calling and to its LORD, must seek to be a light set on a hill, to show the sacrificial love and service that characterised Jesus and that brought life in all its fullness to those whom Jesus encountered and touched and welcomed and ate with and accepted and forgave. In fact, I might go as far as to say that if the ecclesia were indeed like that, then more people might join its gatherings!

So to the devotions of that early ecclesia, we can now turn.

Chapter 2

"Were not our hearts burning within us when he opened up the Scriptures to us?" (Luke 24:32)

The title of this chapter refers to a Bible study that Jesus conducted with two disciples on the road to Emmaus on the first Easter Sunday evening. In my view, it is one of two places to commence the rereading of the Bible in the light of Jesus. The other is the Sermon on the Mount, wherein Jesus explodes the then orthodox understanding, and I might say the prevailing view to this day, of how the Hebrew Scriptures are to be read. For Jesus says several times and quite clearly "You have heard… But I tell you…" (Matt. 5).

Hence in this chapter, in order to reflect upon what it would have meant for the early Church to "devote themselves to the Apostle's teaching", it is from that place on the Emmaus road that we must start. As those two disciples, Cleopas and 'another' walk along from Jerusalem to Emmaus, discussing the extraordinary events the previous few days, their remembrance was, of course, not only of all that Jesus had taught them and modelled to them while he was on earth, but was also the result of the guidance of the promised Holy Spirit, to lead them into all truth. Or, to put it another way, to lead them to Jesus Himself. This is not an uncomplicated process, for the picture presented to us on the pages of the Gospels is of a group of individuals who struggled either to comprehend, or to find it within themselves to want to follow the example and teaching of Jesus, and this was replicated in the life of the early Church.

For the one to whom they were guided by the Holy Spirit, was one who would readily submit himself to the wrath and violence of others and exemplify, most especially in his death that the way to life and peace is through the death of ego. Unless we die to self, according to Jesus, we can never live the full, true, deep quality of life intended for us as human beings, with what Jesus termed an eternal dimension to life, here and now, on Earth. This fullest experience of life in its Hebrew sense, is the idea behind the word Shalom. It will be true of a person who is willing to be self-aware, to integrate their dark side, to be willing to discern the truth of their neighbour and to be forgiving as well as loving towards others.

Moreover, according to Jesus, this neighbour includes our 'enemies', those we find the most difficult, who, it turns out, sometimes reveal that which is generally hidden within the deepest darkest recesses of our 'selves'. It will mean that that person will be willing to see their neighbour's point of view and as in Jesus' case, to have the courage, when necessary, to resist any and every form of abuse of power, whether that be Roman or religious, for the sake of others. It will include a concern for the very Earth itself, as well as the political and economic structures that govern our lives together. During Jesus' Incarnation, this was all too much for the disciples, therefore we should not be too surprised to find that it continued to be so in the experience of the fellowship in the early Church as well as throughout its history.

Jesus' resurrection and His disciples' experience in that upper room, as He expressed his reacceptance of them all, rather than his anger and judgement of them (they who of all people had let him down the most, and who of all people should have known better), these same Apostles were to be utterly relied upon to teach the early Church and indeed us, as we have it recorded on the pages of the New Testament. And we too will struggle, in each successive generation, to come to terms with our own unwillingness and prejudices. For the calling of the Church is to be the gathering of those who view themselves as servants, as those who are willing to die to ego, to love others in the same way, unconditionally, without judgement, but with forgiveness and acceptance, to welcome those whom religious and polite society would deem to be unlovable. And this remains just as much a challenge now as it was then.

So, what I want to attempt in this short chapter is two things. First, and by way of example, to listen in to an encounter between Jesus and a rich, young man, a privileged, and somewhat self-righteous member of the Jewish elite ... and second, to explore Jesus' words to the two disciples on the Emmaus road.

I want to do this to illustrate how Jesus would have us engage with Scripture, upon which he had meditated and based his life and teaching, but which he also so radically re-interpreted. So, let us first attend to a particular encounter between Jesus and a rich young man, recorded for us in Luke's Gospel chapter 18 verses 18-30.

I like to think that their conversation might be expanded thus:

Q: Good Teacher what more can I do to ensure my eternal inheritance?

Jesus, conscious of this young man's attempt to ingratiate himself by his form of address, is nevertheless willing to engage with him, not on his terms, but rather and as always, on his own terms. Of course, Jesus is very well aware that this conversation is being listened in upon, being fully aware of the privileged position that this young man occupies in his community, afforded by money and status. Likewise, Jesus is well aware that for most of those listening, such a question is to one degree or another beyond them, because they are regarded by the religious establishment, as well as by themselves, as not righteous, excluded from Temple worship and the presence of the Lord, and most certainly unlikely to have any inheritance whatsoever.

Jesus notices the emphasis upon the individual personal pronoun, the sense of confidence that this young man appears to have in his own capability, but he also notices the fault in his thinking regarding inheritance, which is only and always a gift, rather than something that anyone could earn. But it would seem that it is the language of money, wealth, insurance and inheritance upon which Jesus will focus the most, since it is from this very material perspective that this young man views things eternal, so Jesus meets him on his own ground, as it were.

According to the religious orthodoxy of the day, riches were a sign of God's blessing, whilst poverty was an obvious sign, either of some form of wrongdoing on the part of those who were poor, or on the part of their parents or their parents'

parents, upon whom God was clearly visiting his wrath to the fourth generation. Not so according to Jesus, who began his first public sermon with the words "Blessed are the poor", and ended it with the words "Woe to you who are rich". The subject of financial inequality, as well as its underlying theological interpretation, seems to have been a very significant reinterpretation, of which this encounter is but one example, in the life and ministry of Jesus.

Jesus decides to work within the framework of this young man's self-understanding, and therefore turns to the Ten Commandments. In the light of Jesus' insight into this young man's wealth and heart, we might have expected him to start with the 8th commandment about theft, but he opts instead for the 7th, the commandment concerning adultery. This too is significant, for adultery was one of the primary metaphors used in the Hebrew Scriptures for Israel's unfaithfulness to God as a nation. Jesus might therefore have hoped that this young man would realise that, and at the same time appreciate how he had distanced himself from this sense of corporate identity. For according to Jesus, he was his brother's keeper as well as his neighbour.

Furthermore, one of the ramifications of great wealth was blindness to the needs of others; blindness to the selfishness engendered by wealth; a lack of compassion and a lack of desire to see justice for all. Indeed, compassion and a sense of justice is what God's inheritance was intended to look like, rather than some individualistic, private possession. According to Jesus, those who were rich, far from being blessed, were thus trapped, as well as being blind to their imprisonment. They, not the poor, would of all people find it the most difficult to believe that the way to peace, shalom, fullness of life, eternity, is not through earthly possessions, but though divestment thereof.

Jesus' choice of the 7th commandment is therefore quite, quite, deliberate. Furthermore, if this young man is wedded to his individualistic and legal mindset, then Jesus' extension of this commandment to include lustful thoughts might also have convicted him. Similarly, Jesus might have hoped that the young man would be convicted by Jesus extending to women an equal right to divorce, women whom he consistently refuses to regard as male sexual property, (which according to the law of Israel, they were), by modelling an alternative and radical way of relating to women.

Beginning as he does, I believe that Jesus' intention is to enable this young man, as well as those listening in, to reflect upon how he regards women, how he orientates his life around property, how individualistically he views himself and his relationship with God and how little regard he seems to have for his neighbours and his collective responsibility, as one to whom much has been 'given'.

So then Jesus reverts to the 6th commandment against murder. Once again Jesus is attempting to enable this privileged young man to see himself as Jesus does. For elsewhere in his teaching Jesus condemns not only violent thoughts towards others but also participation in an Imperial elitist system that maintained an unjust status-quo to the benefit of the few and to the oppression of the majority, including most of those listening in on this conversation. All of this Jesus might hope would occur to this privileged young man as he left pregnant pauses between his reordering of the commandments which the young man will claim to have kept.

Next he turns to the 8th commandment against theft. This includes, according to Jesus, the not so passive participation in an economic system that was so structurally unjust that it rendered the vast majority of people powerless, whilst at the same time enabling the elite few in power to maintain their sense of self-deception, as well as their sense of self-righteousness. And all this whilst turning a blind eye towards their neighbour. This, according to Jesus, was nothing more than a form of false testimony, the 9th commandment. For according to Jesus, in his two commandment summary of the law, the love of others is only ever in the light of the love we have received from God, which we are called on to reflect back towards Him and our neighbour and which is what the 'inheritance' this young man seeks in the future will look like here and now.

However, the real kicker in this dialogue is Jesus' listing of the 5th commandment last. For in the light of this young man's question about inheritance, it is indicative of the depth of Jesus' insight into his primary failing and what is really going on in this young man's heart. For that commandment addresses the honouring of one's parents. It is the climax of the first table of the law which is concerned with our attitudes and behaviour towards Almighty God, who, as clarified by Jesus, is now to be viewed as our Heavenly Father.

Jesus' insistence that God is to be regarded as our, not my, Heavenly Father, enshrined as it is in what we now call the Lord's Prayer (and to which we will turn in a later chapter), was observed by those around him who heard him pray, and was a powerful recasting of God, who was generally understood to be a somewhat distant despot, rather too quick to anger, and for those who viewed themselves as blessed, as righteous, like this young man did, as an avenging angel and warrior Lord who would judge the unrighteous, the unclean and their enemies. According to Jesus, however, Almighty God was much more like a Prodigal Father, whom Jesus described in a parable placed right at the heart of his Gospel, by Luke. This, Jesus might legitimately expect us, at least as listeners, to have in mind –that instead, the prodigal Father, towards this child, whom he has thought dead to him and lost, has only and always been forgiving towards him and abounding in steadfast love and mercy.

Jesus, out of his love and compassion, is determined to continue his dialogue with this privileged, yet blinded young man. And I like to think he continues to offer him, gently, the opportunity to enquire somewhat more deeply into what it is that he is actually asking of Jesus. And so he lists the commandments, which the young man would have understood to have been the answer to his own question, but in an alternative order which is somewhat pointed and certainly intuitively personal. But the young man does not appear to have grasped Jesus' intent, for he responds:

Q: All these I have kept since my (rather privileged) birth (he claims).

Of course in the dialogue as we have it recorded, there are neither rubrics nor narrator's notes to indicate where there might have been looks exchanged, pauses or moments of silence for reflection and wonder, as well as the exchange of looks between those listening in and Jesus, and this young man. So I like to think that Jesus may have paused at this point, or indeed between each of the commandments that he had reordered, in order to give this young man the chance to reflect upon his exaggerated claim.

These pauses, accompanied by Jesus' piercing gaze, might operate to amplify that silence, and magnify the possibility that this young man would see what it was that He was saying, not only about himself, but also by way of comparison, about those around him. I like to think all of this might have been part of their exchange, through words, facial expressions, glances, pauses and silence, the unspoken dimension of their encounter. And one might have hoped that this would have had a profound impact on him.

It seems to me that for those who witnessed it, this encounter would have been every bit as jaw-dropping and heart-burning as that on the Emmaus road. Jesus is challenging the world view of this privileged, yet blind young man. The law, according to Jesus, was only ever an accommodation to the hardness of men's hearts. It was never designed as the means of salvation: for goodness is its own reward, not the means to ensuring an inheritance. That is only and always a gift. Furthermore, what the young man is asking of Jesus needs to be considered in its very temporal, earthly, cultural context. Structural economic oppression and injustice were the order of the day in the Roman Empire, in stark contrast to the alternative Empire which Jesus came to proclaim and incarnate.

In Jesus' alternative Empire, women were equally members of God's family and were not male sexual property. Slavery as THE Roman means of maintaining the economic oppressive status-quo was utterly to be abhorred by those who were to view themselves as equally free sons and daughters of Abraham. So, simply by pausing, Jesus affords this young man the chance to reflect upon himself, his attitudes and the personal benefit he derives from participation in the fruit of the Roman Empire, to the detriment of the majority of others. He gives the young man time to reflect on his selfish attempt to turn salvation and eternal life into something with a monetary value, as if material possessions, rather than treasure in heaven, could ever be the means to life – NOT after death but before death, and NOT for an elite few, but for all!

When Jesus heard the young man's response, and as I say, after a suitable pause, he strikes to the heart of what he has been intending all along and at the heart of this young man who stands before him.

J: Well then let me put it like this. You still lack one thing. Sell everything you have and give it to the poor and you will have treasure in heaven. Then come and follow me.

For those with much to lose this is indeed a hard message, whereas for those with nothing to lose, this is great news. The challenge remains for all who are rich, to hear the words of Jesus in this encounter. Unless we can see ourselves as Jesus sees us, blinded by wealth, blind to the needs of others, blind indeed to our blindness by the cares of this world, our business, our weddedness to status, our unwillingness to divest in order to live towards others in an honourable and respectful way, our unwillingness to allow our ego to be dethroned, we, like he, will never be enabled to follow in Jesus' footsteps.

Unless we die to all forms of self which are so seductive and so damaging to the possibility of an eternal quality to life here and now on earth, we will never experience it, for paradoxically, it is only as we find ourselves to be so identified with others in their brokenness and addictiveness to self, that we will be able to participate in the communion, the fellowship of the broken body of Christ on Earth and together learn how to pray as Jesus did, so that together we can journey towards the new Jerusalem.

Alas for this poor, rich young man, who went away sad because he had such great earthly wealth.

How hard it is for a rich man to enter the alternative Empire (to Rome) of Heaven (here on Earth). It is easier for a camel to pass through the eye of a needle than for a rich man to enter this reality.

When the disciples heard this, true to form, they did not understand. Jesus is using his proclamation about an alternative Empire as being an alternative way to live here and now on Earth and not as something to be viewed as solely concerned with the future, as an inheritance. This mistake is one which so many still make to this day, as if 'salvation', which is how the disciples referred to it, has only to do with some kind of future reward in the after-life, rather than the way we live our real lives now: 'For it is by their fruit that you will know them' (Luke 6:44). How will people know that you are my disciples? 'By your love' (John 13:34), comes the answer. Or as recorded in one of Jesus' final parables when asked when it was that they had practised what he had modelled to them, he replies, 'When you did acts of service to the least of these.' (Matt. 25). Or according to Jesus' brother and one of the Apostles, the truth into which they found themselves led is this, 'Be doers of the Word not hearers only.' (James 1:22) For so-called profession of faith only, without works, is dead (James 2:17).

For Jesus declares at the beginning of his Sermon on the Mount, "Unless our righteousness exceeds that of the Pharisees, the religious guardians of orthodox belief in Jesus' day, we will never enter into the reality of this alternative

Empire" (Matt. 5:20). Unless we can 'see' ourselves and our neighbours recast in the image of our Prodigal Heavenly Father, we will continue to regard Him as an angry, legalistic, hard hearted, avenging God. We will never be enabled to regard Him through the eyes of a little child, while we continue to hold onto a view of ourselves which is rooted in law-keeping, reward and punishment, clean and unclean, slave and free, male and female, status and achievement, us and them, and will miss out on the experience of the fellowship with and interdependence upon, this Prodigal Father, in prayer, as the broken body of Christ, while here on Earth.

Jesus confounded all their religious categories and expectations. In this one dialogue, this one encounter, we can read all that was on Jesus' heart and all that was in this young man's heart. It is for this reason that it is always dangerous, in my view, to stray too far from the pages of the Gospels where we encounter Yahweh, the Lord, Jesus, face to face. To stray into other portions of Scripture, especially some parts of the Old Testament, not in Jesus' company, is a perilous, dangerous and potentially fatal business. For the record of Ancient Israel's projections of vengeance, wrath and violence onto God, in their desire for deliverance, is all too plain.

So, second, I want to attempt a somewhat whimsical retelling and expanding of the encounter between those two disciples on the road to Emmaus that first Easter Sunday evening. On that road Jesus recasts their Scriptures to such an extent that, 'their hearts were burning within them'. Jesus recasts the entire history of his people, as it was recorded in the Hebrew Scriptures, from his perspective as the forgiving victim, from the perspective of those who are sinned against, for listeners who need to experience the joy of undeserved forgiveness and of being brought home on the Good Shepherd's shoulders rejoicing.

He thus reveals Himself to them as the promised suffering servant, the anointed Christ, High-Priest of God most High, who would offer himself as THE acceptable sacrifice, once and for all and always replacing the blood of animals, and as a judge, chosen (like those recorded in the Biblical book of that name), who would not wreak vengeance and bloodshed upon others, but lay down his own life as THE final declaration concerning such bloodlust; "It is finished" (John 19:30).

So now we must turn to that Bible study on that road, and endeavour to hear Jesus' recasting of that record. Let us turn to Luke chapter 24 from which the title of this chapter is taken. I like to think that the monologue might have gone something like this:

"How foolish you are and slow of heart not to believe that the Son of Man, whom Daniel saw at the right-hand side of the antecedent of time, is the sovereign LORD of all history. The one to whom all judgement was passed, the one whom the Father loved, the I AM, the LORD, who is in the Father and who is one with the Father, who came into the world not to judge the world, but to save it from itself and to seek and to save the lost.

How foolish you are and slow of heart to believe that the Son of Man, who saw the fiery throne of the living God, whilst He may have thundered his warnings to his people throughout their history, would ever write them off and start again. The LORD could never leave his people desolate, even though his servant, Ancient Israel, his first-born son, had been so unfaithful and failed to practise justice. No, because of His name, He would not treat them as their behaviour deserved, but instead would put his Spirit within them, resettle them and build a new Temple in their midst that would be named "The LORD is there" (Ezek. 48:35). And from that day, there would be no more death, no more mourning or crying or pain, for when the Son of Man was lifted up, He said: "Behold I make all things new" (Rev. 21:5).

How foolish you are and slow of heart to believe, that I AM, the LORD, who appeared to Moses in the burning bush and to Daniel's three friends in the fiery furnace. For I AM the one who delivers from slavery and death. It is for freedom that I have set you free, not so that you could once again return to a binary way of thinking, that would exclude this person and judge that, but so that you could live in the 'at-one-ment' of all things and all peoples, no longer living in fear of the projection of God that you have made for yourselves, but rather living in the security of my abiding love.

You may have heard, "An eye for an eye and a tooth for a tooth", but I tell you I AM, not the Angel of death but the LORD of life, abounding in steadfast love. So I tell you, "Love your enemies", do not return tit for tat, but treat others as you would like to be treated. Don't think that forgiveness runs out at seven times, but go on forgiving "seventy times seven", for this is what your Father in Heaven is like!

The only sign I would give you was that of Jonah, who in his sectarian small mindedness knew, deep down, that I AM, a gracious and compassionate God, slow to anger and abounding in steadfast love. One day the city of Nineveh will be destroyed. That must happen because the city represents man's collective resistance to the good and gracious purposes of God. Men must therefore be separated from the city if they are to dwell in the Heavenly Garden City. Yet, because I AM the creator of all things and all peoples, even the hated and detestable Ninnevites are my beloved children too. Poor Jonah, he so hated knowing that truth deep down, but credit to him for his honesty in recording his anger and projection onto a God he cast in his own image, who would avenge and punish those others that he thought deserving thereof.

But my Empire is not like the Empires of this world, that have come and gone, all built on greed, injustice, slavery and violence, even the one established by my servant David, but rather they are like the Empire ruled over by his son Solomon, the Prince of Peace. I could take no delight in murder and adultery, but am always ready to forgive and once my prophet Nathan had opened David's eyes to his self-righteousness, his deceit and his self-reliance, he knew in his heart the assurance of my love for him, which had never ceased.

But do not let yourselves be deceived into thinking however, that repentance is a prior condition of my love and forgiveness, or that it is something that qualifies you and not others, as if one of God's children could ever be preferentially treated over another. No, repentance is the realisation only ever after restoration, only ever after the homecoming, that you have always been loved, that you could never not be loved and that nothing within you or your circumstances could ever separate you from my Father's love.

For I AM, the LORD, your Creator and your Redeemer and though you may continually choose to live individually enslaved to your desires and passions and imprison yourselves and others in fear and shame, I am still your Redeemer. Though you may choose to live in cities that only serve to confirm this resistance to God's goodness and grace, collectively and institutionally, whilst at the same time blinding you to what you are doing, I will still be your Creator. I AM, the Deliverer, who has paid your ransom and set you free. One day you will see this.

I AM not the angel of death, or a God who desires destruction, or who punishes out of wrath – do I have to repeat? I AM, the LORD of life, the beginning, the end, the first the last, the one by whom all things were made, and in whom all things hold together, the light and life of all humankind, the Word made flesh, who with and in the Father, is eternally present and who now will make that reality available to all people. Not only have I been through the curtain in the Temple as High Priest, but that curtain was my very body, now torn from top to bottom as the final sacrifice, so that all creation might be permeated by the reality of forgiveness and the renewal of life today and every new today, for evermore.

How foolish you are and slow of heart not to believe that my embrace, my covenant, would reach out to all peoples, the first and the last, the least and the lost and include women and men equally. Ruth the Moabitess, who according to the law, should have been excluded from the household of faith alone, is presented as an example of faith and faithfulness that rivals even that of our forefather Abraham, which, considering all her cultural disadvantages of nationality, status and gender, is remarkable. Even Abraham believed that my Father would require the sacrifice of his beloved son Isaac, as though my Father needed to be appeased, as if my Father would ever require the taking of a life. So what joy was Abraham's when our Father provided a temporary alternative animal sacrifice and Isaac his beloved son was spared.

So consider the destitute widow and foreigner Ruth, or Rahab the prostitute and Tamar, who also had to prostitute herself with her father-in-law to obtain justice, all icons of inclusion, forgiveness, redemption and grace and that that alone is the will of our Father. And that is why these women will be included in my genealogy, when Mathew records it. Or consider Esther, who was willing to submit to becoming one of the women in the Lord of all the Earth's Harem, Esther who was elevated to the status of Queen, who became God's High Priest, and as such so courageously mediated and pleaded for her people, even risking her own life. Her people's peril had resulted from a quarrel between two proud men, the one stubborn, and the other jealous. Have you not read that it was on the third day that she accomplished the salvation of her people? Was there ever a clearer forerunner in all the Hebrew Scriptures, and she a woman acting as High Priest? Can you not see that the crib, the cross, the empty tomb and the garden are the Holy of Holies, the place where I AM, High Priest and sacrificial lamb, the scapegoat and THE At-one-ment, made once and for all?

Or Cain, that first murderer, that first city builder, who set this whole sorry story in motion. For even he was given the mark of the cross on his forehead as a sign of God's protection. My prophet could see it: "The LORD demands mercy not sacrifice" (Hosea 6:6). The sacrifice of self out of love for the other, not the sacrifice of the other for the sake of self, or tribe, or nation or the myth of redemptive violence. Violence will only ever beget violence, it cannot produce lasting peace. And now I have broken that cycle once and for all. I have revealed the scapegoat mechanism for what it is, the darkness in all humankind. And I have revealed its alternative, the self-sacrificial love that alone truly makes for peace.

How could my people have been so blind as to think that they were chosen over and against other peoples, rather than for and on behalf of them? They were chosen to be a light set on a hill to show the nations the way that leads to life and peace. How could they ever have been so misled by those same nations as to believe that the way to peace could ever be attained through the sacrificial blood of others or that their God was like the Gods of the nations and demanded such blood?

Now surely they will see that my blood is the last blood to be shed in sacrifice, my and my Father's accommodation to the misunderstanding and darkness in men that demands such murder and bloodshed in the name of a God cast in their own image. Now the character and will and purpose and heart of their God is once and for all made known. For now my blood, the blood of the suffering servant, the great High Priest, is sprinkled over all the nations. Now it has been revealed that God is not a God of wrath, God is not set over and against the peoples of the Earth, nor has he a favourite nation or one which elevates men over women or one in which the first are preferred to the last. No, in his Kingdom, all that is reversed. Now the last shall be first, the lost shall be found and women shall be my witnesses and Apostles. All shall be welcome at my Heavenly feast. The table is now laid and ready.

How could they now not see that my only and abiding resistance is to their resistance of me and my grace, love and forgiveness? How could they not now follow my example of inclusion, acceptance, forgiveness and welcome, as I sat and ate with sinners? For surely when they do this, break bread and pour out wine, whenever they gather around a table together, they will see themselves as they truly are, both sheep and goats, both susceptible to the darkness as well as indwelt by the light. Surely, as wine is poured out and bread broken, they will recognise me in that moment, in those elements, in one another and in all the world?"

So, it seems to me that Jesus wants us to reflect upon what we are hearing in the light of his incarnational bias to the poor, and his identification with the victim. His own willingness to suffer men's anger, abuse of power and bloodlust, is the revelation of what God's judgement looks like. Thus, he shows that judgement is the separation of our true self from all that which binds us to a variety of false views of self. And this he did in complete contradiction of the then normal understanding and expectation of a condemnatory, even vengeful judge. For Jesus is willing to be judged, to be condemned by men, rather than to condemn, and in so doing He reveals the forgiveness and grace of God. This is the judgement for which He came into the world.

And all this He does so that we will not make the same mistake as they did, which is to turn the Good Shepherd of the Gospels into the ravenous wolf of judgement awaiting us in death and at the end of time. Our predisposition to project our fears, anger and demands for justice onto the living God, and to recast him as a God of punishment, violence and destruction seems to me to be just as pervasive and dangerous today as it was then. Moreover, it is a complete misrepresentation of the good news of Jesus and his reinterpretation of ancient Israel's Scriptures.

Jesus is revealed as the descendant or seed of Abram, himself the descendant/seed of the firstborn son of Noah who had survived the flood, which had consumed the entire known world, as the one through whom, "All the nations of the earth will be blessed" (Gen. 12:3). For the Lord God had promised never to destroy the world again but to find another way to separate men from their collective resistance to him represented by the city. And that way of deliverance, begun in the choice of Abraham the Father of the nation Israel, would be fulfilled through his seed (singular), as the Apostle Paul so delightfully puts it (Rom. 4:13), in Jesus' deliverance of all peoples.

This Jesus, rather than as anticipated, and let us be frank, hoped for, did not come as a terrifying Judge to wreak vengeance and wrath upon those with whom he was not pleased, but rather as the one who would become the object of human wrath, would be murdered and yet breathe forgiveness and peace upon those responsible, commissioning them to do the same in his name, and to the ends of the earth, rather than replicate the emissaries of Rome and the myth of redemptive violence, that the orthodox interpretations of Scripture, not only in Jesus' day but ours, would have us believe.

Jesus retells their Scriptures to them from the perspective of the despised minority, that of Isaac, the one so nearly sacrificed according to the religion of the day, but rescued from that fate by Yahweh, Jesus; from the perspective of Jacob the jealous, deceitful, younger son without inheritance, from that of Joseph, the hated favourite son of his father, sold into slavery, wrongly imprisoned and yet elevated to the highest office, who chose not to wreak vengeance upon his jealous and murderous brothers, but to demonstrate love, forgiveness and generosity.

Jesus retells their Scriptures from the perspective of a slave people whom Yahweh, Jesus, rescues from their oppression in Egypt and leads to a land of promise; from the perspective of one who does not quote from the books of Joshua and Judges and will not be identified with the genocide recorded there, but who, having been given the name Jeshua, 'Deliverer', undertakes that task not through violence and bloodshed, but by being willing to lay down his life in self-sacrificial love.

He takes the perspective of those disenfranchised by the Law, those excluded from the Temple by virtue of being unclean, those labelled as unrighteous, as a loving and forgiving Father, rather than a somewhat brutal and demanding dictator God. His perspective is that of a Creator God who has the wellbeing of all his children at heart, rather than a self-regarding sectarian few; a God, who, whilst He may have chosen to reveal his purposes through a particular somewhat oppressed people, (a people with nothing especially to recommend them, not powerful or prodigious), ancient Israel, always had the welfare of all nations in His mind and on His heart.

This sectarian, ethnically determined and limited vision of much that passed for the orthodox interpretation of their Scriptures in Jesus' day, and tragically too often still in ours, was something that Jesus had to completely dismantle on the road that day and that remains the task of the fellowship of the church today – to go on recasting the Hebrew Scriptures from the perspective of Naboth, rather than the King who would have stolen his vineyard; from the perspective of Nathan who requited King David for a similar crime; from that of the wisdom rather than the decline and corruption of King Solomon; from the perspective of the Son of David, the Prince of Peace, rather than that of David, who was celebrated for being greater than Saul because, "he killed his ten thousands and Saul only his thousands" (1 Sam. 18:7/ 29:5), and remained a warrior deliverer; from the perspective of the prophets who 'saw' that the bloodshed of either animals, in Temple sacrifice, or of humans in warfare, had never been God's intention. "I desire mercy not sacrifice" –quoted by Jesus twice for emphasis in case we missed it (Hosea 6:6/Matt. 9:13/12:7).

The suffering of God's servant is the means to redemption rather than vengeance.

Chapter 3

To the Fellowship
"All the believers were together and had everything in common…giving to anyone in need." (Acts 2:44/45).

The early 'Church' devoted themselves to 'the fellowship', as a nascent sect, within their established religion, which was deeply rooted in their Jerusalem Temple festival attendance and their local Synagogue. In this chapter I will explore the components of the continuity and discontinuity between what would become the two cousin religions of Judaism and Christianity.

According to the last verse of Luke's Gospel, Jesus' followers' practice was to go to the Temple to worship, and they are there once again on the day of Pentecost. Peter's sermon that day has a considerable impact upon the Jews who had gathered there for the feast, resulting in a large number of people coming to some form of realisation that this Jesus, whom they had so recently crucified, was indeed the anticipated and promised Christ of their God, Yahweh.

The affirmation, "Jesus is Lord", would become almost the byword of belief amongst this early community of followers of Jesus, this 'messianic' sect, within the established religion of their day. They would rapidly become a persecuted minority by that religion and over the forthcoming years, disputes between this minority sect and its parent, majority religion would result in a huge gap in belief opening up between them.

This in turn would result in the editing of the Jewish Scriptures, such that in their established form, those Scriptures would have lost many of the proof texts that the early Christians used within their religion to prove that Jesus was not only the Christ but also the Lord. The word 'Lord' is the English translation of the Greek for 'Yahweh' in the Hebrew Scriptures; this 'Yahweh' who had periodically appeared to his people throughout their history.

Apart from the priestly cast, who maintained the Temple and thereby their power, most Jews regarded the Temple, which was destroyed in AD 70, as corrupt. With its destruction, what was in the process of becoming Judaism, and which we now regard as the ethnic religion of Jews, parted company once and for all with this new sect, which we now refer to as Christianity.

Thus this early Fellowship was a fellowship of those who had found themselves compelled, by their experience of the person of Jesus, or the conviction of His Spirit, to come into a relationship with the God of their Scriptures, Yahweh, the Lord, who, in the person of Jesus, had appeared in the flesh, and who now, after his resurrection and ascension was seated at the right hand of the Almighty, the unseen God most High of their Scriptures and who now, by his Spirit, is everywhere present as the light and life within ALL humankind.

It is not my place here to explore how such extravagant convictions and affirmations might have become so quickly established amongst this small but growing nascent sect, but this was the basis of their fellowship: that Jesus is not only the Christ of God, but the Lord of their People's history, as recorded in their Scriptures, and furthermore that this Christ, having been crucified by those to whom he came, breathed forgiveness and peace upon those first disciples, those who were most guilty of betrayal and yet who, remarkably, were now called to be his Apostles, THE messengers, par excellence, of the gospel, the good news of God's love and grace to all peoples.

That this was an extremely difficult message, not only for their fellow Jews, but for these nascent 'Christians', is borne out by the early chapters of the book of Acts. The first Gentile seeking to be baptised into this Fellowship is a black African eunuch, whom the Law of Israel was quite clear about excluding; "No one whose testicles are cut off or whose penis is cut off shall be admitted to the assembly of the Lord (Deut. 23:1). The law could not have been clearer and yet here was the authority of the Spirit of Jesus extending that fellowship way beyond anything they could readily accept, although in the light of Jesus' earthly ministry, this should hardly have been surprising!

The opening up of their religion, not to mention the reinterpretation of their Scriptures, could not have been more clear, nor the universal embrace of the good news that they had come to put their trust in, nor the fact that it had now been extended beyond law-abiding Jews, not simply to include Gentiles, but those Gentiles who most certainly could not be regarded as God-fearing in any technical sense.

Whilst on Earth, Jesus garnered a reputation as a friend of publicans and 'one who ate with sinners and tax collectors' (Mark 2:16). He was willing to touch lepers as well as dead bodies, three of whom He raised to life. He allowed himself to be touched by women and most significantly, women of a particular reputation. He conversed with a Samaritan woman of ill repute in public, whilst he also became known as a glutton and a drunkard (Luke 7:34).

That by his Spirit, therefore, he should have chosen an Ethiopian Eunuch as an icon or window for the early Church to have their eyes opened to the sovereign and universal extent of his love and grace, should not have been a surprise. But of course for those enculturated Jews, born and brought up under the yoke of the Law of Moses, to take upon themselves voluntarily such a cross-cultural alternative yoke from Jesus, was extremely alarming and most certainly challenging.

Two chapters later in the book of Acts, this message is underlined and confirmed through a vision to Peter, the rock on which Jesus had prophesied the early Church would be built. The inclusivity of his vision and his calling to embrace the Roman centurion Cornelius, who was an archetypal representative of the Roman Empire, the total opposite of that which the earthly Jesus proclaimed and incarnated, would have been very shocking indeed, hence the need for it to be given to Peter of all people. If this Gentile of all Gentiles could be included within the fellowship of that nascent Fellowship, alongside another Gentile who incarnated the very antithesis of purity, the Ethiopian Eunuch, then no one was beyond the embrace of God.

Once again this should have been no surprise to Peter or to that early Fellowship in the light of their experience and observation of Jesus' earthly ministry. For this Jesus could say of the woman whom he had healed, who had been bent over for 18 years, "This woman is a daughter of Abraham", much to the chagrin of the synagogue ruler that day (Luke 13:10-17). The significance of the 18 years being that in the book of Judges, to which this period of time refers, Jesus is casting the woman in the role of Israel, bent over by foreign oppression and the synagogue ruler as that oppressor who would exclude her from the fellowship of her people. NOT so, according to Jesus.

Or several chapters later, Jesus invites himself to Zacchaeus the tax-collector's house for tea, again to the chagrin of the rest of the population of Jericho where he lived and who hated him for his compromise with their Roman oppressors, for his cheating, swindling, abuse of power and greed, yet Jesus describes him also as a "Son of Abraham" (Luke 19:1-10). No one, it would seem, is beyond the reach of Jesus' embrace within the household of Israel, neither a disabled woman, nor an unclean tax-collector, two graphic examples to law-abiding Jews, of Jesus' blatant disregard for the Law of Moses. And then, by way of further abhorrent extension to his principle of inclusivity, neither an Ethiopian Eunuch nor a Roman centurion, both Gentiles, are to be excluded either!

And to make this as clear as day and beyond dispute, in Peter's vision, recorded in Acts chapter 10, he is addressed three times. This must have been especially painful to Peter, who, as Jesus had predicted he would, denied Jesus three times prior to his Crucifixion (Matt. 26: 69-75),and who had been asked three times, after the Resurrection, on the shore of Lake Galilee, if he loved Jesus (John 21:15-19).

In this vision, three times, he is addressed by the Lord and encouraged to kill and eat an animal that is unclean, in complete contradiction of the Law of Moses, only to be reprimanded and told in no uncertain terms, "Do not call anything impure or unclean that God has made clean". And in case we might be tempted to restrict the meaning of this vision and these words to food, it is further confirmed to Peter that we are 'not to call anyone impure or unclean'. With Peter concluding, "I now realise that it is true that God does not show favouritism, but accepts men and women from every nation".

The Apostle Paul too, in his letter to the Romans, repeated and explored God's seeming lack of discrimination and lack of favouritism (Rom. 2:11) and goes on to show that God's Covenant with Abraham has now been extended beyond ancient Israel to include all nations, who may equally look to their forefather Abraham for their covenantal inclusion (Rom. 4). And he universalises this still further in the following chapter when he says: "If through the act of one man's disobedience, sin reigns in death, how much more can we say that through the actions of one man, grace reigns through righteousness to eternal life" (Rom. 5:12-21).

With the conclusion of his doctrinal thesis, Paul confirms that whilst God's people, ancient Israel, may have stumbled, using his metaphor of a race, they have not fallen beyond recovery, and will complete the race alongside the Gentiles (Rom.11:11). For the current disobedience of ancient Israel has resulted in the mercy of God being extended to the Gentiles who had also been disobedient, so that God might have mercy on all peoples, first the Jews and now also the Gentiles. He follows this up with a doxology in praise of the depths and riches of the wisdom of God that the abundance of his grace and the depths of his mercy might be extended beyond God's chosen people, ancient Israel, to all peoples, in fulfilment of his covenant with Abraham. Abraham, the chosen instrument of God's grace to rescue all nations and all peoples, who in different ways and at different times were all as guilty as one another of disobedience and equally undeserving of God's abundant grace (Rom. 11: 28-36).

This fellowship then, which these early Christians sought to practise, was no easy thing. They were being called to live openly towards others and especially towards those whom their very upbringing had required them to exclude as unclean, impure, alien and indeed as enemies. They found themselves being called to be an open Fellowship under the yoke, not of Moses, but of Jesus, putting their trust in a man whom they had experienced as THE 'enfleshment' of Yahweh, the Lord, the Son of God, the Christ, and whom they would rapidly come to see also as the Wisdom, the Word, the beginning and the end, the creator of all that is, unseen and seen, who by his Spirit was enlightening, empowering and guiding them into the truth and into fullness of life. The truth was that this same Jesus, who by His Spirit, continued to convict them of their own spirit of exclusion and judgement of others, as well as their projection onto others and even God, of their fears, anger and shame. The truth being that this same Jesus, shone the light of his presence, by his Spirit, into those dark places of their lives, in which they were blind to that spirit of prejudice and exclusion, and to their own guilt.

The members of this Fellowship required a massive re-education of their understanding of what it meant to be a child of God, to be a son or daughter of Abraham, whose family had not simply been enlarged to include those within their midst, who they had previously viewed as unclean and untouchable, but also to those beyond their ethnicity, unclean and impure Gentiles. And of course that impulse to exclude, to judge, to label and not to accept or welcome, is alive and well within us all and of course within the Church of our own day. It would seem that the constant thread within Jesus' teaching, calling us not to judge, but to seek to remove the log within our own eye before ever we turn to the speck in our brother's eye (Matt. 7:5), is tragically as necessary today as it was then. Jesus constantly wrestled with the Jewish religious leaders of his day, the guardians of orthodoxy, those who interpreted the Law of Moses in the restrictive and exclusive way that they did, and the need to wrestle in the same way as there is for us in our present day church too.

Again we should not be surprised by this. If Peter found it so difficult, then why would we not? So the challenge for those early Christians in their Fellowship, was constantly to walk in the footsteps of Jesus, to be open, welcoming, inclusive and not judgemental. The idea that there might be conditions, qualifications or rules that would guide our perception of, for example, who might be welcome at the Lord's table, seems a far cry from both Peter's vision and from the witness to us of those whose company Jesus sought while on Earth, and yet too often that is what we find to be characteristic of the Church today.

The start of Philip Yancey's book *'What Is So Amazing about Grace',* records the story of a teenage girl who has become pregnant. Thrown out of the family home by her parents, she eventually finds her way to his church. He asks her why she has not come sooner, for by this time she is desperate. Her response is tragic and salutary for those of us who are members of the church. She simply says that what she expected from the church was more of the same, namely judgement. It had never occurred to her that she would experience anything else.

And that is truly tragic, because I have more than a sneaky suspicion that her expectation, as well as her story, could be replicated over and over again. Most people today would not regard the Church as open, inclusive, welcoming and accepting, but rather as the opposite. The Church today has drifted a long way from the experience of that early Fellowship recorded for us in the book of Acts, struggling though it may have been with the revelation of the extent of God's grace and mercy!

What then are the threads that we might draw from this brief survey of the experience of that early Fellowship of both the life and ministry of Jesus and of his Spirit in the early chapters of the book of Acts?

1. That this Fellowship is called to be an open-ended and inclusive one, the very opposite of a closed religious group with qualifying conditions, whether that be on the grounds of ethnicity, doctrine, caste, gender, sexual orientation, disability, social status or any other line that human beings like to draw in the sand between 'us' and 'them'. For as someone famous once said, the moment we draw such a line, Jesus is on the 'other' side of it!

2. That this Fellowship will be characterised by the same reversal of values that we see in Jesus' ministry. Again and again he elevates the least, the last and the lost at the expense of those who regard themselves as the great and the good and the first. It is the Spirit of the song of Mary:

1. "He has been mindful of his lowly servant, and has scattered the proud in their conceit.

2. He has brought down the mighty from their thrones, but has lifted up the humble.

3. He has filled the hungry with good things, but has sent the rich away empty".

4. This captures the spirit of what Jesus incarnated and that which the Church is called to model itself upon in each particular day and age.

3. That this Fellowship actively seeks to expel all categorisation, whatever that may mean in each day and age, so that no one should ever feel that they are impure or inadequate, disqualified or unclean and most certainly not an abomination. For we are now no longer under the yoke of Moses, but the yoke of Jesus, for whom even our perceived 'enemy' is our neighbour as the story of the 'Good Samaritan', a contradiction in terms for Jesus' audience, so expertly puts its finger on. 'You may have heard, love your neighbour and hate your enemy, but I tell you, love your enemy and pray for those who persecute you' (Matt. 5: 43/44). No wonder the powers that be hated him; he spoke with authority to rival that of Moses!

4. In our previous chapter we looked at the Apostle Paul's teaching, and how he grappled with Jesus' reinterpretation of His own people's Scriptures for Gentile congregations, which brought him into conflict with Peter. The challenge which that early Fellowship faced, remains to this day. It is to read the

Hebrew Scriptures as Jesus read them, with a most certain bias, and a freedom that expresses the 'oneness' that we all now have in Christ. For in Christ there is a celebration of personhood and uniqueness without the hierarchical labelling element so prevalent within us all. For now in Christ there is no condemnation. We are all one and there is 'neither Jew nor Greek, neither slave nor free, neither male nor female, for we are all one in Christ' (Gal. 3:28).

5. That this Fellowship seeks to 'see' the extent of the grace and mercy of God expressed in the life, ministry, death and resurrection of Jesus, as present always and everywhere, in and for all peoples. That they seek to recognise and embrace that which was alien to them and yet was evidently the work of God in the lives of others. This calling is to be the Fellowship of those who would not restrict the presence and work of God in his world to the Church.

6. Whilst the Church may be a light set on a hill, a sacrament of the presence of God in the world, it does not have exclusive claim to the Spirit, presence, grace, mercy or activity of God in His world.

7. So one obvious and classic example of this would be to see, in the life and work of Gandhi, someone who walked in the footsteps of Jesus and yet who died a Hindu. This Fellowship was being encouraged to see that their experience of God could be the experience of others who were very different to them and yet were experiencing the same God, recognising an equally authentic expression of God's grace and peace.

8. That this Fellowship, on the basis of God's covenantal dealings with humankind, both in Abraham, to whom the promise was made that through his seed, God would redeem all nations, and thus, in and through the second Adam, would include all peoples within the embrace of God's grace and mercy, children of the same Heavenly Father.

9. This too remains a challenge for all religions and sadly also for many traditions within the Church to this day. The idea that all peoples are already God's children, whether they acknowledge that parenthood or not, is for many, heresy. However, it seems to me, that to suggest that unless and until someone conforms to some form of entry requirement, they cannot be regarded by 'us', as members of 'our' Fellowship, seems to be a radical departure from the practice of Jesus while he was on Earth and a departure from the purpose of his vision to Peter. Surely it is a form of judgement that we are called to deplore, it is a fresh embrace of the yoke of Moses, and the heresy or false teaching that this early Fellowship was constantly wrestling to avoid, as must we.

10. That this Fellowship will inevitably be difficult and require all those present to be willing to suspend years of prejudice and fear, as regards 'others', and to seek to work out their differences around the Lord's table.

I have three pictures of this Fellowship, the meaningfulness of which will appeal in differing measure to different readers:

One is the Sunday lunch table at which four generations of family gather, aged from zero to 95. Their conflicting agendas and abilities, stories, hopes and fears, all contrive to make agreement even about the order of events, or its location, let alone menu, fraught. Nevertheless because we are family, that is what we do and we believe that it is a good thing to rub one another's edges off in a spirit of love and acceptance. There is a willingness to say sorry, to be forgiving and to be regularly reconciled to one another after yet another fallout. That at least seems to me to be why much of what we now call the New Testament was written, to churches struggling to get along with one another, with all their differences, around the Lord's Table.

The second picture or term is that of 'Messy Church', which we host here in our church building a couple of times a term. It is essentially for small children and their parents and guardians. It always strikes me that the banner we display in the week leading up to these events really ought to be left up permanently, because that is what Church inevitably will be. Not in the sense of plenty of glue, paint, bubbles and pasta, but in terms of people's messed up lives.

More often than not, church gatherings are characterised by people wearing their Sunday best, in some degree of pretence or another, and by pleasant conversations rather than real, honest, vulnerable, and soul searching ones. But if Church is genuinely to demonstrate an alternative to the Empire of Rome, which was rooted in class distinction, status, greed, power and oppression, rather than the recognition that we are all equally messed up in different ways, it needs to be immediately clear to everyone present and to anyone visiting.

It is not the quality of the worship or the preaching that will recommend the church to those seeking an encounter with the living God, but rather the honest telling of the stories of those who gather, in the light of the story of God's involvement in the messy business of living on Earth, in the person of Jesus; His willingness to suffer as the victim of male anger, was in order to show us that there is another way to peace, through our willingness to express our fear, shame, anger and guilt, as we find ourselves to have been welcomed into his loving arms, and in like manner to welcome others.

If the Church was able to be messy, to be genuinely honest about its failings and faults, rather than to seek to cover them up, then others might just be enabled to see that Fellowship as the light set on a hill, as a real presence in its community and as a real and viable alternative to whatever the current form of Empire has to offer, which is always more concerned with appearance, reputation, success and power.

The third picture that I have in my mind, in order to understand what this Fellowship would look like, or indeed how it would be experienced, is an AA gathering. I was privileged enough to attend a couple of meetings with a friend some time ago. I have to say that their gathering in my experience came closest to what I understand the Fellowship that is being described in the New Testament to be, both in terms of its reality and its aspirational calling to incarnate an alternative way of being which is not judgemental or exclusive.

There were a number of reasons that I believe I experienced such a depth of fellowship at these AA meetings. Some might argue that such a 'fellowship' is merely horizontal and lacks the vertical dimension or sense of the transcendent that any church gathering ought to manifest, whereas as I have observed, and have come to appreciate, this line from '*Les Miserables*' is profoundly and deeply the truth, "To love another person is to see the face of God". Human beings in all their brokenness, their mess, their pain, self-loathing, anger and frustration being honestly and vulnerably expressed, is the place wherein the real presence of the divine is most evident.

The AA meetings that I attended began with each person simply stating their first name, no titles, no status awareness or differentiation, followed by an open acknowledgement of their addiction, in this case to a particular substance, but in all our cases to a way of being that is self-destructive and destructive of harmonious human relatedness. Each person was then warmly and genuinely greeted by the group, whose non-judgemental welcome and acceptance of them as an equal member of a group of addicts was heartfelt and deeply touching to me. Then together the steps were rehearsed which for all the world seem to me to be like a discipleship programme, a fellowship group of mutual support, interdependence, vulnerability and conscious and articulated acknowledgement of our individual and collective need of God, a higher power, that which is beyond and within us all.

As the prologue to John's Gospel says, '… the light and life of Christ within us all', which I would seek to affirm in a church gathering, such that together we recognise our need, turn together towards the one who walked this road before us and eat and drink around His table, feeding upon him in both Word and Sacrament. Thus it is that as his broken body on Earth, we can be remembered (as our liturgy reminds us week by week) and go back out into our daily lives to live in an alternative way that demonstrates that peace is wrought through self-sacrificial love, acceptance, lack of judgement, and vulnerability. This is the honest expression of brokenness, in imitation of Christ, so that others whom we encounter may dare to live in this liberating way as well.

So I want now to attempt to redefine several of the words that I have used in this brief survey of the experience and struggle of this first Fellowship as they were coming to terms with the teaching of the Spirit of Jesus, who was seeking to lead them not only into the truth, but also into fullness of life; a life that welcomed all peoples as equally beloved members of God's family, rather than excluding them on some basis or another, for sake of the maintenance of a particular social order or status quo. For this Fellowship was truly both an alternative to the Judaism of its day, as well as to the patriarchal elitist structure of the Roman Empire under whose influence it was called to live.

If the yoke of Moses was particularly prescient to this early Jewish sect, so too was the yoke of Rome, if for different reasons. This early Fellowship was called to live under the yoke of Rome as an outpost or sacrament of an alternative Empire, characterised not by violence, privilege, oppression, slavery and suffering, but by equality, sacrificial love and forgiveness; such characteristics fitting for those called to follow in the footsteps of the One who was willing to lay down His life in the face of the wrath of men and to bring an end to the myth of redemptive violence. Pax Romana was precisely that, a myth, and real and abiding peace, the peace of Christ, could only be established through the same self-sacrificial love that Christ demonstrated.

The first is the word '**church**' which we often use today to describe a building, but which is actually one further degree of separation from the meaning and freight of the word the first followers understood and intended it to mean, namely, to describe themselves. The two words used in the Hebrew Scriptures to describe the gathering of the people of God were the Greek words from which we have derived Kirk (ekklesia in Greek) and Synagogue (sunagos in Greek).

This early Fellowship wanted to affirm their continuity with the story of God and his manifestation throughout the Hebrew Scriptures to his people in the person of Yahweh, the Lord. Obviously, synagogue was already taken, so they took the other. At the same time of course they were inevitably in conflict with their established religion Judaism, which regarded them as an heretical sect.

Thus from its earliest days, this Fellowship was seeking to be BOTH continuous with His story of the salvation of all peoples through the person of His Christ, His servant, His High Priest, His Son, the Lord AND to distinguish themselves from the religion that had birthed them, which wanted to maintain pride of place in the purposes of God, to hold fast to the Law of Moses and to restrict membership of the household of God via ethnicity.

At the same time, the word **ekklesia** also meant in their day simply 'a gathering' and would have been understood in that way by Gentiles and so the gathering of those seeking to follow Jesus would also be a counterpoint to the gatherings of those often in the Temples of their cities, that functioned not simply as places of worship and revelry, but also as banks, stock exchanges, market places and public meetings. Their choice of the word **ekklesia,** now our word 'church', was therefore both what we might term a religious expression, as well as a statement about the public truth of their experience of Christ, as affecting every part of their lives and not just their religious or spiritual lives. It was rather a counter-cultural, economic and political choice, all of which I am afraid is lost on us who simply use the word church to refer to old buildings!

The second word that it is important to have an alternative grasp of is the word '**orthodoxy**', which for some is an expression of creedal conformity, for others liturgical correctness and for others Biblical inerrancy. In fact the Greek word doxa means 'glory' and to view the word as meaning 'correctness of worship' might be a more helpful way of understanding it, unless of course we are of the view that worship is something that certain people do in certain buildings for a limited period of time during the week, in the case of Christians, for an hour on a Sunday morning.

In fact, worship has to do with the direction of our lives, that which is central to it, around which we orient our time, talents and energies. Worship is an all of life commitment that may be focussed around a table where messy stories are shared and addictions acknowledged, but ultimately worship is how we live out our lives each minute of each day, as we rub shoulders with others and either live according to the regime of Rome, or in our case, that of Capitalism and the worldwide web, or the reign of Christ. For despite appearances to the contrary, Christ has conquered all worldly forms of Empire, however beguiling, seductive or attractive they may seem, and by his example of self-sacrificial, forgiving, non-judgemental, and accepting love, offers us an alternative, and that is our real, every day, everywhere worship.

The third term that it would be good to understand a little better is the word '**religion**'. It has had a bad press recently and is possibly irredeemable, and with its history of the persecution of minority groups, its abuse of power and its more recent cover-ups the institutional church has cast a dark shadow over the Christian religion. The word actually means to 'religament' us. I see this as meaning that through certain practices (for example those of the AA programme), and as expressed through the liturgy of the church as it gathers, we can be put back together –'remembered'.

Furthermore religion is not a once and for all done deal, but is all about developing alternative, good habits. It is the ongoing practices of those who know that they are only ever recovering addicts, and that they are only ever one step away from another plunge, that they are never, this side of the grave, ever fully recovered.

So the final word that requires a fuller understanding is the word '**liturgy**'. Once again this is a word that has had something of a bad press, in that it has come to be associated with a form of church practice that is either dry, out of date, irrelevant or hypocritical. It simply means 'the work of the people'. It is what those who gather do when they get together. To use the picture of the Sunday lunch table therefore, it means that there are diverse responsibilities as far as preparation, the laying of the table, the shopping, the cooking, the serving, and the etiquette surrounding the eating goes, as we genuinely encounter and connect with one another around that table.

It is the forms of words that we use as we gather, as we greet one another, as we share our commonality and human identity that includes the wellbeing of those who are not present, as much as it includes those who are. It includes too a sense of thankfulness and wellbeing as a result of all that the planet so bountifully provides for us, as well as the One who stands just behind the veil and sustains all that s/he has made good. It affirms that shared vision of the peace of Christ and how that is to be accomplished on Earth, as it is in heaven.

It includes the confession of our addictions, the affirmation of our absolution and the empowering sharing of our stories in the light of THE story of our liberation, in and through the broken body and poured out blood of Christ, as well as our sharing in that feast at that table, our prayer as Jesus taught us, that is only and always about all God's children and must never become a private form of devotion only.

Thus, as that Fellowship gathers (church) and does its work (liturgy) together, those who participate have the chance at least to be remembered (religion), at least for another week, so that they may live their lives (worship) orientated around its source in the person, example, teaching and sacrificial death of the One who holds them and all things together, and who is the real presence and being encountered in many places always, everywhere and in all peoples, to His praise and glory (orthodoxy).

Chapter 4

"He took bread, broke it and their eyes were opened and they recognised him…"

(Luke 24:30/31)

These words are taken from the conclusion of the encounter between the two disciples of Jesus on the Emmaus road after they had invited Jesus into their house to eat with them. In this chapter I want to consider the third thing that those early followers of Jesus devoted themselves to, referred to in that text as, "the breaking of bread".

Elsewhere it is known as the Communion, the Eucharist or the Lord's Supper. It is probably the thing that has caused the most internal division within the church throughout its history and certainly was of central significance at the time of the split in the Western Church during the Reformation. In the Roman Catholic Church there is the doctrine of transubstantiation, by which it is understood that the bread and wine become the flesh and blood of Christ, indeed the Eucharist is the central rite of their liturgy, with considerable emphasis placed on the role of the priest, who re-presents Christ's self-sacrificial offering of himself at the altar.

In non-conformist, Protestant churches this rite and this doctrine were resisted, and in its most minimalist form, the

Communion service was but a memorial of Christ's death, whilst the role of the preacher, rather than the priest, was central and the preaching of 'the Word' and the Fellowship of the church, of greater importance than Communion. We see here the same divide as we saw in the early Church, between Jewish and Gentile forms of experience and understanding of the Gospel, received from their respective Apostles, as well as the same level of conflict, sadly, that they also experienced.

Within the Anglican Communion, because of the way in which the Church was established in this country at the time of the Reformation, both of these wings are held in an uneasy tension, the one evangelical, emphasising the Bible, preaching and preacher, and the other Anglo-Catholic, emphasising the Eucharist, the liturgy and the priesthood. Personally I want to be greedy and have both, believing that the verse we are attending to in this book, as well as the experience of those two disciples on the road that day, hold both together. Indeed I would go as far as to say that the way in which Luke constructs the telling of that story, as well as where he has placed it as the climax of his work, suggests that to divorce and separate these two wings within the church is a grave mistake.

In the Lord's Prayer, Jesus encourages us to ask our Heavenly Father to: "Give us today our daily bread". As a sentence and indeed as a request, this has lost much, if not all, of its significance to those of us who live in the West, owing to our relative affluence. I would suggest that amongst those of us who use the Lord's Prayer in this part of the world, there is very little sense of our daily interdependence, either with those who live elsewhere or in our community or indeed with creation itself, which provides the essentials necessary for our bodily survival.

Apart from a relative few in our affluent society today, most of us need give little thought to the idea that we may not have enough to eat today or tomorrow. The early Church accrued a reputation for being a company of those who, unlike many around them in those brutal days, would care for their neighbours who were suffering and in need. It certainly remains the case that those in need in our country today ought to have confidence that their local church will similarly be a place of succour, and that the service of that church is not restricted to an hour on a Sunday morning!

We only need to turn on the news to appreciate the extent of the need in our world today, the suffering of those who have so little and to witness the structure of the world economy, which means often that the agricultural produce of the two thirds' world, is harvested at a price that leaves many of those who have laboured to produce it living at or below a subsistence level. And that is before considering the environmental factors and risks of disaster which limit longer-term sustainable life. This is reprehensible and insupportable and of all institutions, the Church is called on to address this.

But for now, our attention is on but one line in that Lord's Prayer, which has been set by Jesus, I believe deliberately, in a Eucharistic context, and is not dissimilar to the line quoted by the writer to the Hebrews from Psalm 95: "Today if you hear his voice harden not your heart...", requiring us to focus our attention upon today. THE issue now, for both wings of the Church therefore, must be the impact of both word and sacrament in the lives of those who gather week by week. We need to ask, is the Church being fed *daily* by every word that proceeds from the mouth of God (Matt. 4:4/ Deut. 8:3), as this quotation from the lips of Jesus, in his encounter with God's prosecuting Angel, Satan, in the wilderness, bids us? And are we feeding on the flesh of Jesus, who is the bread of life, and drinking his blood (John 6:35/53 and John 15:1)? For according to Jesus, unless we do so, we can never enter the alternative Empire of Heaven that he came to make present.

Today

That 'today' is every day. It is here, and it is now. Eternal life, which Jesus said he had come to bring, is NOT something for the future but for the present. Similarly, Heaven is NOT somewhere else, for the Kingdom of Heaven is 'in your midst' and 'it is within you', says Jesus. Whatever else is being undertaken at Communion therefore (and there is plenty else as we shall see) is for us, and it is here, and it is now.

That 'today' of which the Scriptures speak so powerfully and eloquently is the present reality in which God abides always, time being merely something that he has given us to enjoy and to appreciate and within which we may accomplish that to which we are called, and to which we shall return. But the presence of God is something to be appreciated, enjoyed and celebrated always and everywhere and by all peoples, as our liturgy reminds us again and again. For God is eternally present within us, if only the eyes of our hearts could be opened like those of little children to that reality. And that is what the Communion service is designed to accomplish.

It replicates the actions of the High Priest in the Holy of Holies, that place which represents the reality of God, "in the midst", of the Temple, which itself represents the entire creation. The 'at-one-ment' accomplished by the High Priest, now fills that creation, as the veil of that old earthly temple, Christ's body, is torn once and for all, so that all may now participate in the life of God, by eating his flesh and by drinking his blood. That reality is the reality of day one, that first day of creation, 'IN the beginning', according to the account in Genesis.

This truth that was with us from the very beginning of time is now present to us in our experience and especially so in this sacrament. In and through this rite, the remission of sins, the renewal of the entire creation and the restoration of the eternal covenant are accomplished, incarnated and made manifest to us. This is indeed a Holy mystery. For that at-one-ment, that communion is between God and all that he made good, and over which he appointed a High Priest, an image bearer, Adam, both male and female, called to till and to serve in the paradise, the garden of God. This is our great calling, our great joy, to be privileged to participate in the 'today' of God, and which the Communion service celebrates.

Bodily

What is at stake is our spiritual wellbeing, but even to express it in this way is to suggest a split between the soul and the body, which this sacrament of bread and wine does not, in my view, suggest. What is at stake is therefore not our spiritual wellbeing but simply our wellbeing; to split off our spiritual health from our physical health means that we miss the bodiliness and earthiness of the Eucharist. This is something that this sacrament will not let us lose sight of. Elsewhere the Apostle Paul will suggest that offering our bodies daily is what our true spiritual worship is (Rom. 12:1). His theology is rightly, deeply rooted in Jesus' incarnation.

There is something utterly earthy, practical and physical about our humanity that this sacrament will not let us lose sight of, despite the propensity of both wings of the Church to do so, turning our worship into something that primarily has to do with our souls rather than our bodies. Daily feeding upon the bread of life and drinking from the true Vine, is more than just a reminder of our bodiliness, it is a necessity for wellbeing, for all round health, for 'shalom', for peace. For without an awareness of our bodiliness, and that of our neighbour, we cannot appreciate the full extent of our interdependence with one another and with the entire creation.

It would seem that there is an urge within human beings to pander to some kind of religious or ascetical hierarchy; it is almost as though there is a form of 'spiritual' snobbery, an unwillingness to get our hands dirty, which is so great, that the thought of actually washing someone else's feet is appalling to us. But that is precisely the context in which Jesus instituted this 'sacrament', and it is to such earthy, practical, daily service that his example and the entire burden of his teaching calls us.

Whether we like it or not, whichever wing of the Church we find ourselves in, life of and in Christ is messy. In our previous chapter we considered what the constituents of such a messy church might look like. During the sermon at a recent Eucharistic service at St Paul's and at a particularly poignant moment, Terry's dog, who had accompanied Terry to the service, decided to sneeze. We all paused thinking it was a one-off sneeze, but several more followed! Whatever the moment had been, it was lost and had become something else.

When said dog had finished I said, "Bless you!" and we continued. As a congregation we might wish this had been different, we might wish that Terry, who has been homeless and suffers from mental health issues, who often appears on a Sunday morning drunk and whose language can be extremely colourful, might stay in bed. We might wish he was more reverent, that his dog might not precede him to the Communion rail or indeed be present at all, but we refrain.

And we encourage ourselves in the thought that this is the LORD's house and the LORD's table and that all are welcome and that this sacrament is one of the 'bodiliness' of Christ as well as ours and that bodies are not always dressed up, washed, clothed acceptable, healthy and tasteful, but are often none of these. Terry is an icon in our midst for our own relative degree of bodily unacceptability. Terry gives us the opportunity not to judge, not to be too precious, and not to lose sight of who we are as human beings who have both souls and bodies. This is not easy, it remains a challenge, to make all welcome, but it is necessary, and it enables us not to lose sight of the ordinary, bodily, messy nature of the context and essence of our gathering as the broken body of Christ and therefore, of course, of the sacrament of Christ's broken body.

Hospitality

If the first aspect of the Communion service is that it is earthy, messy and has to do with our 'bodiliness', then the second aspect needs to be the context from which this sacrament sprang, namely a meal. And before I talk briefly about the particularity of that meal, it is important to put it in its wider context within the public ministry of Jesus. The

Gospels confirm the importance of the ancient sacred duty of sitting and eating with others, the offering of hospitality. The centrality of this to Jesus in his ministry and it being at the heart of what it meant for God to be incarnate, is also equally evident on the pages of the Gospels. For Jesus not only met and ate with his disciples, and those with whom he was most intimate, for example in the home of Mary, Martha and Lazarus, but he also accepted the invitations of the religious leaders, the Pharisees. Indeed so central was this to Jesus, that it resulted in him garnering a reputation as one who, "sits and eats with publicans and sinners" (Mark 2:16), a "glutton and a drunkard" (Luke 7:34)!

Somewhat strangely, it was only as we as a church attempted to practise hospitality, that we discovered the theology that underlies it. It is not simply one way in which we seek to love our neighbours, to provide meals for those who would otherwise not have a home cooked nourishing meal, (true though that is), it is THE ordinary, everyday, messy, place where we can, if we take the opportunity, stop, sit, gather, take time, talk, share, serve and be served. It is THE place where relationships can develop, where we can become known, where we can be heard, where we can share our stories, feel understood, feel accepted and loved as we are, for who we are.

This is of course sometimes a challenge in terms of who is at the table, their manners, their eating habits, their language, our judgement, our sense of self, who we think 'we' are and who we think 'they' are. Indeed, someone once said of these occasions, "You cannot tell the doctors from the patients", and that is because the meal table is a leveller. This was Jesus' milieu: for encounter, for conversation, for building, establishing and sharing in relationships.

The meal table is THE multi-generational centrepiece and gathering place for a household, for a family and for the Church. In its original context, it is not a place of restriction or of formality, but a place of informality, of discovery, of acceptance, of laughter and tears, of the sharing of our lives with one another. Hospitality is at the very heart of Jesus' expression of the reality of God being with us, in and through his Incarnation.

Liturgy

I want now to turn to the particularity of the meal at which Jesus instituted what we now call the Communion service, the Eucharist. For Jesus deliberately staged this meal to coincide with the Jewish feast of the Passover. It is therefore understandable that many associate Jesus with the paschal lamb, sacrificed in order that the Angel of Death might pass over the households of the Israelites whose doors were daubed with the blood of the lamb. However, the Passover sacrifice is the one offering that is not presented by a priest.

And whilst the writer of John's Gospel wants to make it clear that Jesus is the Passover lamb, both at the beginning of his Gospel, in John the Baptist's recognition of Jesus (John 1:29/35) and at its end, by assuring his readers that none of Jesus' bones were broken (John 19:26/Ex. 12:46), it is in the very breaking of the bread that the sacrifice which Jesus fulfils, is recognised. And that is the atoning sacrifice made by the High Priest once a year in the Holy of Holies.

The New Testament confirms this interpretation of Jesus' actions, because by far and away the largest body of texts alluded to or directly quoted from the Hebrew Scriptures, centre upon precisely these two aspects of what it was that Jesus accomplished on the Cross, namely his role as High Priest in the order of Melchizedek, and his fulfilment of the prophecies of God's appointed suffering servant and sacrifice, promised by Isaiah.

So it is to these that we must turn in order to explicate what it is that Jesus may have imagined he was instituting at the Last Supper and that we now celebrate in the Communion service. For according to Jesus himself in Mathew's Gospel, the new covenant which he was establishing through his death on the Cross and making real by his presence in and through the bread and wine of Communion, was not the covenant the LORD made with Moses on Sinai, the Covenant of Law, but rather the covenant he had previously made through Noah with the whole creation and which would be renewed by the Lord's servant (Isaiah 49:8) on the Day of the LORD, the Day of At-one-ment, the eternal covenant, the new covenant promised by Jeremiah (Jer. 31:31-37) and by Isaiah (Isaiah 61:1) for the forgiveness of sins (Lev. 25:10/Matt. 26:28).

Acting as High Priest, Jesus would sprinkle his own blood (Isaiah 52:15), rather than that of a bull (Lev.16/Heb. 9:12), both for the remission of sins and for the renewing of the entire creation. Jesus was a High Priest in the order of Melchizedek, who had appeared so mysteriously without genealogy and human descent, to offer Abraham bread and wine and give him his blessing (Gen. 14:8). He was the fulfilment of a Heavenly Priesthood, vastly superior to that of Moses' brother Aaron, who was of merely human descent.

Jesus, as THE suffering servant, was THE sacrificial offering (Isaiah 53:10) upon whom was laid the sins of all (Isaiah 53:6/9/Lev.16:21), THE scapegoat which was sent out into the wilderness on the Day of At-one-ment.

This was how the Apostles explained Jesus' role to the new Jewish converts. Moreover Paul, the Apostle to the Gentiles, adopts the same approach when he quotes from an existing and early Christian hymn (Phil.2:6-11). He views Jesus as the promised suffering servant who, like the High Priest, having once made the sacrifice for the propitiation of the sins of both Jew and Gentile (Rom. 3:26), is highly exalted and proclaimed as the Lord.

Thus both prodigal, younger (Gentile) brother and firstborn, and eldest (Jewish) son are God's beloved children. Both are welcome at the feast, since all that the Father has is theirs and always has been. It could not be otherwise, for now that all have fallen short, neither son is righteous, each has turned to his own way (Rom.3:10-12) and yet 'in Christ' all now have access to the throne of grace. And most delightfully, the first Gentile 'convert' turns out to be a black African (Ethiopian) eunuch, one whom the law of Israel permanently excluded from the Temple (Deut.23:1), but who is now embraced, as we might have expected, in the light of Jesus' earthly ministry of inclusion. He is one of those whom the religious 'system' would have excluded again and again and again.

This sacrament, is therefore, a liturgical re-enactment of Jesus' inclusive embrace, of Jesus' words of welcome, of Jesus' presence in us and to us and for us, always and everywhere, here and now, in and through bread and wine at table and altar, as we sit and eat together. I might not be able

104

to say that the elements become the flesh and blood of Christ, i.e. by means of transubstantiation, but equally I could not say that after the words of invitation and invocation they remain merely bread and wine. For something mysterious is happening here at this table, at this altar.

I need now to make a slight technical detour in order to attempt to draw out the liturgical threads of this mystery. There are four key words that are both historically and liturgically relevant and need some explication, all of which are rooted in the rite of the At-one-ment and the role of the High Priest in the Temple. When the High Priest emerged from the Holy of Holies, as the Lord for the day, having performed the rite, he was greeted with the words that accompanied Jesus, as he rode into Jerusalem on what has become known as Palm Sunday: "Blessed is he who comes in the Name, the Lord" (Luke 19:38/Psalm 118:26).

As hopes for Jesus' imminent return to Earth dimmed, the word that had expressed the hope that he would come, **"maranatha"** (Rev.22:7/12/20), morphed into an understanding of their experience that the Lord would come in the Eucharist, (finally written up in John's Gospel). This hope was then expressed in the Communion service, by the invocation **"epiclesis"** that either the Holy Spirit or Jesus himself would come upon or into the elements of bread and wine.

As those elements are lifted up and consecrated, they become, as it were, mysteriously, Jesus the Lord, enthroned as both High Priest and sacrifice, both Son of God and slain lamb, and the **"apotheosis"**, the God becoming, has occurred. This replicates the experience of Moses and Solomon, for example, who witnessed the glory or the presence of God, filling both Tabernacle and Temple (Ex. 40:34/ 1Kings 8:11). In Christ, the High Priest has now come once and for all and completed the atoning sacrifice in his own blood, for the forgiveness of sins and the renewal of the entire creation.

In Luke and Paul's accounts of the Last Supper, they use the word "**anamnesis**" (Luke 22:19/ 1Cor. 11:24). The translation of this word has sadly been the cause of much dispute. It can be translated as either, "in memory of me", favoured unsurprisingly by the Reformed, 'memorialist' wing of the Anglican Church, or "invoke me", favoured by the Anglo-Catholic wing. This word is a recalling of the person of Christ to be present through the bread and wine.

When the Priest re-presents the bread and wine at the altar/table in the Eucharistic liturgy and lifts them up, they become (apotheosis) Christ's body and blood. The priest remembers (anamnesis) Christ's passion and invokes (epiclesis) the Holy Spirit to come (maranatha) so that the veil, which hung in the Temple, and which is Christ's flesh (Heb. 10:20), torn once and for all in the moment of his death, might be removed from our hearts and minds, and the glory of the Lord be manifest through the elements of bread and wine, to those who are gathered and for those who are not.

This desire, hope, and liturgical act is reflected in the Lord's Prayer (to which we shall turn in our next chapter), in the line, "Your alternative Empire come". The prayer of the follower of Jesus is that Jesus will be present in, to, through and for him or her. It is a prayer that is answered, I would say, in all sorts of ways and in a variety of places, because it is Christ, both Jewish and Gentile Apostles assure us, who indwells everyone and who holds all things together. Therefore, through the torn veil in the Temple, the glory of the Lord has entered into every nook and cranny of the entire creation, with the Eucharist as the living picture of this.

This appreciation of the presence of Christ through a liturgical act is the work, as we have seen, of all people, always and everywhere, for they are, according to both Jewish and Gentile Apostles, all 'in Christ' and Christ is in them, a royal priesthood, no less.

When they gather at the Lord's Table, the priest re-presents, on their behalf, the sacrifice of Christ that is completed by their daily worship and their recognition of Christ's presence every day, everywhere and in everyone. In that moment, in that gathering and through these elements, the Sacrament is not merely an act of memory or of something that happened in history or that we look forward to being fulfilled at some point in the future, rather, it is the focus of, and re-presentation of, our real encounters with Christ, and the means by which we are forgiven and re-membered.

As the wine, like his blood, is poured out, and the bread, like his body, is broken, so we are fed and enabled to become the broken and blessed body of Christ poured out for the life of the world. We might even say that as the expectation that the Christ would return to Earth as a man soon receded, so the understanding that the primary way in which the Christ would 'come' to us on Earth in the meantime, would be no less real or powerful and would be *experienced*. Luke records that this is just what the early Church devoted themselves to – the Apostles' teaching, the Fellowship, the breaking of bread and the prayer.

Communion

Perhaps it is rather too obvious (yet I feel it is needful) to say that the Communion service celebrates the communion of ALL those who gather, as well as (representatively), those who do not, the community of the entire creation. It includes the communion of saints, those who have died and gone before, but even more than that, it also manifests an eternal reality: Jesus is the lamb who was slain before the foundation of the world (Rev.13:8) and thus he has accomplished what might be described as a cosmic reconciliation of all things in and to himself (2 Cor. 5:9/ Col. 1:17/20). The Communion service, then, celebrates the communion of God him/herself, Father, Son, and Holy Spirit, in whose plural, yet singular, male as well as female, image we are cast.

This means that none are excluded and more positively, that all are included, unless of course they self-exclude. But even more than that, what is being celebrated, and we trust experienced and glimpsed through the liturgy and the gathering, the eating and drinking, is the union that lies at the heart of all things, for that is the essence of what it means for God to be God, in whom there is both plurality, diversity and yet oneness.

And this is crucial if we, as those who gather, (as those who are church) are ever to overcome our human propensity not just to exclude and judge, but to project that differentiation onto the person of God, who has gone to such great lengths to enable us to move from binary thinking, seeing and behaving, into unitive thinking, speaking, behaving and living. For in Christ there is now neither Jew nor Gentile, slave nor free, male nor female, for all are one in Christ (Gal. 3:28) who is God. It is a complete contradiction of our faith and the word

Christian, to differentiate between 'us' and 'them'. "Give us"… all of us, for we are all God's beloved children, whether we know it yet or not… "today our daily bread".

Architectural

I want now to take a slightly different tack for a moment, but one that I believe illustrates well the two different traditions within the institutional Church and their respective Jewish and Gentile Apostolic legacies. When the church building of which I am the vicar was built in the early years of Queen Victoria, its construction was rectangular with a pulpit and pews. It was modelled on the synagogue and designed for teaching and preaching purposes. By the end of the then Queen's reign, the chancel and two transepts had been added, so that the building was then in the more 'normal', traditional and certainly more recognisable, cruciform shape, modelled on the theology of the Temple, the place of sacrifice, in Jerusalem.

These were not insignificant nor neutral architectural statements. The original concept for the building was evangelical, its development Anglo-Catholic. To this day, literally, the building has gone on being redeveloped to meet the needs of the community it seeks to serve. The preacher now is no longer six feet above contradiction, with the congregation in serried ranks listening to a monologue. The Priest no longer presides at Communion at a high altar below the east window, with his back to the congregation, in replication of the High Priest in the Holy of Holies, where none but he dare go.

We now sit as neither synagogue nor Temple, but rather as ecclesia, church, as the new Heavenly Temple of Christ's broken body on Earth. We sit around the Communion table, a visible icon in our midst, of the presence of Christ whose sacrifice avails for all. On that table are always the cup and the chalice, whether we are to celebrate Communion or not, a lighted candle and a cross on a table cloth appropriate to the church season. We gather together around that table week by week as a royal priesthood, each in his or her own way contributing to that gathering and participating in the liturgy, being held, represented, and mediated by, with and for the priest of the parish, to whom that privilege, honour and service is given by those who gather, as well as by the wider church, who have recognised his or her calling to that particular service.

All has been done, with a circular seating arrangement and the redevelopment of the structure of the building, to honour both the calling of the Priest to the Priesthood, as well as his or her calling to research and expound the Scriptures on behalf of the people of the parish, whether they are there or not. Thus, the reality that all who are in Adam are now also in Christ, that all may now draw near to the throne of grace, that all are welcome, that all are members of God's family, and that all are members of a royal priesthood, is honoured.

Personal/Relational

Our circular seating plan, with the chairs arranged around a central table/altar, is of course not to everyone's liking, but what would be? The seating arrangement means that we are all unable to avoid looking, at least at some stage, at one another. It requires us to see and to witness the reality that we are the broken, blessed body of Christ poured out for the life of the world. As we gather week by week we cannot help but see in the faces and in the bodies of those who gather, evidence of the journey of their lives and of our journey together.

As we all now face one another around the table/altar, kneeling and with empty hands outstretched, we glimpse the deep connection between the at-one-ment wrought by Christ once and for all on the Cross, the deep at-one-ment between us, who experience various degrees of brokenness in our lives, and the deep at-one-ment between us and all peoples and indeed the planet itself, which goes on experiencing the pains of childbirth, until 'that final today', as the Apostle Paul puts it, 'when all shall be one', or as Mother Julian puts it, "All shall be well".

We witness week by week how the sacrificial love of Christ is being replicated in small and various ways by those who kneel. We witness how, in almost imperceptible steps, those who kneel are glimpsing the reality of Christ's sacrificial love for them, and their Heavenly Father's love in sending him, a love that gradually, over the weeks and years, transforms our joys and sorrows into treasure in the clay jars that we are. There is a line in a Leonard Cohen song that talks about the cracks in the jars letting the light in. My impression over the years, as week by week we kneel together around the Lord's Table, is that it is through those cracks that we are all enabled to see the light within each of us shining out.

As we receive, as we eat, as we drink, week by week, looking at one another, our sense of interdependence cannot but grow, as we allow ourselves to be touched by one another.

111

Our sense of our need of grace cannot but grow as our lives are laid bare before one another. We cannot but experience the transformation promised to those who seek to take up their crosses and follow Christ to the Temple in Jerusalem, to die to ego, and take His life into ourselves; He who is the bread of life and the true wine.

Heavenly

Those who gather week by week around that table do so not only for themselves, but also representatively, for that gathering represents those in the parish who do not attend. It is not only the focus and replenishment of those whose lives are daily being outpoured and broken, but also of those who have gone before, with whom they join. Furthermore, our daily worship on Earth represents and joins with, the worship of Heaven, which is continuous: "On Earth as it is in Heaven". For we join in the heavenly affirmation in the company of Angels and Archangels, as our liturgy confirms: "Holy, Holy, Holy, Lord, God of power and might, Heaven and Earth are full of your glory, Hosanna in the highest!" and "Blessed is he who comes in the name of the Lord", words taken from the book of Revelation and the Psalms.

The coming of Christ is neither mere historical remembrance, nor only a future prospect, but rather a present reality, "Maranatha, Come LORD come" (Rev. 22:20), in the lives of those who gather, in our world and in our worship.

Missional

Our gathering is neither merely memorialist, nor idle future dreaming, but rather with a view to action and service.

We are recalled to go in his NAME, to offer our lives as holy and acceptable to God which is our true worship, to fulfil the mission of the Church, which the Anglican Church has so delightfully summarised thus;

1. Serve our neighbours
2. Love one another
3. Care for the environment
4. Seek just institutions
5. Share our stories

Week by week we recognise our failure to do these things and how little impact our faltering steps towards the New Jerusalem make in our world. Nevertheless, as year proceeds to year, there are signs in different people's lives of the fruit of the indwelling, or I might say the ingesting, of Christ. This is not some religious act that we engage in around the Lord's Table, of some individualistic or private benefit (though that it may be). No, this is a meal with a view, this is the renewal of our calling to action and service, to recognise the needs of others, to love the unlovable and those we find the most difficult in our midst.

This is a call to join with others in the care of our planet which is under threat not least from plastic bags! This is a call to stand alongside others in the name of human rights, justice and peace in our world. And this is a call to encourage one another in that service; to say, authentically, vulnerably and honestly how it is being the broken body of Christ in this place, week by week by week. This is a call to be church, focussed in our weekly gathering together around the Lord's Table, like those at an AA meeting who welcome one another unconditionally, as wounded addicts, as those who are in need of grace and one another, to make it through the week; that we might reflect the reality of heaven, where all is at one and all is at peace, where there are no more tears and no more death. This is our hope and our hearts' desire as we come forward, kneel, hold out empty hands and are given the cup of blessing and the bread of life.

As we receive the body of Christ, so we become the body of Christ in this place and for those communities within which we live. Unless the bread is broken, it cannot be shared and unless the wine is poured out, it cannot be drunk. The degree to which we are willing to enable one another to share our weakness and interdependence, will be the degree to which the sacrificial love is experienced in our midst.

The danger is that forms of religion, ritual or sound teaching, depending on which tradition they belong to, will only ever be theoretical food. For the Communion bread to become the bread of life and the Communion cup to become a cup of blessing, then our brokenness must become the hallmark of any gathering of what is called church, if it is to be a witness to the presence of Christ in and through and for all things and all peoples.

Political

So finally let me say this, there is more than enough food in the world for all the planet's inhabitants to be fed. What is lacking is the willingness of those inhabitants to share the riches of God's bounty and grace equitably. We cannot eat and drink at the Lord's Table without being reminded of the needs of our brothers and sisters across the globe, who hunger and thirst for food as well as for justice, every new today.

We are therefore to be mindful of all our neighbours who are our responsibility in some measure and of our Heavenly Father, before whom we are accountable for our actions towards others, who are more than our neighbours, but rather our brothers and sisters. Jesus pronounced woes upon the religious leaders who had made their religious observance exclusive, and were responsible for closing the door of the Temple and the worship of God to the vast majority, either by their restrictive definitions of God's holiness or by the burdens of debt that the economic structure of which they were beneficiaries, imposed.

According to Jesus, riches were NOT a sign of God's blessing but rather a stumbling block to those who would seek to enter into his alternative Heavenly Empire, in which there is equality and justice, compassion and forgiveness for all, symbolised so powerfully by Jesus' table fellowship. The Communion table of all places, therefore, must be a visible sign of God's justice and of his desire that all should experience the great Jubilee of remission of sins, and of restoration to family inheritance, wherein all may sit, eat and enjoy the fruit of their labours.

To come to the LORD's table is to hear his voice today beckoning us to follow in his footsteps as those who, having eaten his flesh and drunk his blood and thus received his life (John 6:53), are willing to pour out our lives for the sake of others, for the sake of justice and peace and for the sake of all, whatever their ethnicity, their colour, their creed, their gender, their age, their ability or their sexual orientation. For bread is a basic necessity; all must eat to live. We must not presume upon the grace of God in such a way as to turn this sacrament into a religious act that loses sight of the basic human needs and rights of all God's children to sit and eat at his table, at his altar.

As one of our liturgies says: "Come, you who have much faith, you have little, you who have tried to follow Jesus and you who have failed, come you who hunger and thirst for richer life and for a fairer world, come. It is not the priest who invites you, it is the LORD who invites you, for this is not the table of the church but of the LORD, so come".

Chapter 5

"LORD teach us to pray, like John taught his disciples"
(Luke 11:1)

I want in this chapter to explicate the Lord's Prayer, by way of taking up the last of those things listed in Acts 2:42, that is, prayer, to which the early Church devoted themselves. I feel it is necessary before I do so, to make some introductory remarks on the subject of prayer. For it seems to me that what is generally understood and seems to be the accepted orthodoxy within and outside the Church on this subject, is dangerous and fallacious.

It is believed that if we pray hard enough, if we believe hard enough, if we are holy enough, righteous enough, devout enough, and are law abiding, then God will answer our prayers. I have expressed it in this rather caricatured way to help us to see just how erroneous such a view is, even though it would seem to be, as I say, the prevailing understanding.

I remember that when my grandmother became really ill and I had recently started attending church, my parents, who did not then attend church, asked me to pray for her recovery. Despite my prayers, she remained unwell. Not only did my faith in prayer diminish drastically, but my parents' view of my new found faith was confirmed. It was empty and ineffectual. Perhaps, as they suspected, there was no God, for if there was, He most certainly did not seem to care about my grandmother. Or perhaps it had to do with the condition of the one praying, her grandson, who had so confidently assured his parents that because of their lack of faith, because they were not Christian, God would not listen to their prayers! Perhaps this grandson's profession was spurious, or inadequate. Perhaps that was where the fault lay.

Either way, my grandmother continued to be unwell. The response of the church that sometimes God wants us to wait or that sometimes his answer is "no", were far from comforting, especially when this God was compared to an earthly father, who would of course give his child what he needed when he asked, in this case the restoration of his grandmother's health. Something needed to be adjusted if my faith was to survive, since clearly prayer did not work. A few weeks later, having given up on praying for her, my grandmother got better, possibly according to some in the Church to whom I talked, as a result of my hitherto 'unanswered' prayers.

I needed to re-evaluate what I understood by the word 'prayer', and I believe so does the Church. I believe that is why Jesus gave us His teaching on prayer, to dispel the false illusion of a slot machine view of God and prayer, which seems to be so prevalent. Little children are immediately attended to by their parents, who as far as they are able to, meet their needs, salve their wounds, gather them up in their arms and provide the necessary comfort. Not so once those children have become adults. And the Lord's Prayer is most definitely for the adult children of their Heavenly Father.

Around the same time, my wife and I had started a family. We sought to provide each child with all the necessary creaturely comforts, including the security of our presence. Yet, night after night, as we prayed for sleep, we prayed in vain! Then randomly, suddenly a decent night's sleep would come out of the blue, tempting us into a false hope that it would continue, only for us to find it was a one-off and sleeplessness returned. As far as I could see, asking for a night's sleep is not too far removed from asking for daily bread.... In our case, none was forthcoming.

Of course that then begged a number of questions, for the view of prayer with which I had been furnished, was not only mechanistic, a slot machine version of prayer that had little to do with the relationship between a parent and a child, but was also rather individualistic and potentially sectarian, as though the God in whom I believed was only interested in answering the prayers of certain of his children, rather than all his children, of whose needs he is most assuredly aware. If Jesus bids us address a loving heavenly Father, this is not someone who requires conditions to be fulfilled, this is someone who loves both prodigal son as well as hard-hearted elder brother, this is a God who will not disinherit, who has no favourites and whose gracious and merciful purposes embrace all his children, whatever their religious orientation may or not be.

This will be a heavenly Father who hears the prayers of all his children, wherever they may live and whatever their circumstances may be. And this must mean, if He is to be viewed in any way as God, that He cares as much, if not more, for those millions of people in the world who may or may not say the Lord's Prayer, and yet who are daily denied food, as well as justice. Those millions who, as a result of the structural economic injustice in the world, experience shortage each and every day of their limited life expectancy, of which the members of my little family are the passive beneficiaries, living as we do so comfortably and in such privilege here in the West.

So the answer to this prayer, if it is to be called prayer and if God is to be called God, must include ALL his children, whose earthly, as well as heavenly, inheritance is every bit as much as theirs as it is mine. This ultra-Western, mechanistic, individualistic, sectarian view of God and prayer simply will not do, indeed it suggests a view of a God who is particularistic and who favours some of his children over others and who is somewhat and more than a little temperamental and vain, rather than a gracious God, abounding in steadfast love for all his children.

Having said all that however, perhaps the most useful piece of wisdom I ever heard on this subject, was provided to me by a friend in the Church, who somewhat exasperatedly, finally said to me, "Well if Jesus prayed, then so should we". And that really got me thinking, because I could not get past the fact that it was Jesus' practice, alone and with his friends, in the synagogue and in the Temple, in private and in public, extemporaneously and liturgically… to pray. I had to go back to the drawing board.

What I realised was that Jesus' public ministry was bracketed by two bookends of prayer, the one in the wilderness and the other in Gethsemane, both of which were private, but which He must at some point, and with particular purpose, have communicated to his disciples. It is not my purpose here to go into the particulars of the vision that Jesus was provided with in the wilderness, nor of his awareness of the presence of Angels. Nor do I want to suggest that the anguish of the Son of God, on two such unique occasions, wrestling on Earth with Satan as He was, was in any way transferrable to us as God's children on Earth, however much we may feel tested, accused and tempted at times.

Rather, what I believe Jesus communicates through his experience in prayer, is that as God's beloved children, as those who are 'in' Christ, as those in whom the Spirit dwells, we too can have the same confidence that Christ had in the outcome of our wrestling in prayer. For Christ did not seek or accept the easy path, the immediate answer, the provision of bread, the power that would one day be restored, or the glory that He had once had, but rather He was willing to wait in trust upon His Heavenly Father, who would lift Him up and give Him a name that is above all names. But this was only as he was willing to walk through the valley of the shadow of death, to be lifted up on a cross and to experience in his death the full extent of His oneness with His Father, to show us that the death of ego, the separation from the flesh, all that resists the loving and gracious purpose of God in our lives, is the only true way to life and peace.

Jesus' willingness to trust, to wait and to wrestle is our pattern in prayer and, as He would go on to teach His disciples, the Holy Spirit is the answer to all our prayers. Therefore, His presence in us is all we need to go on trusting in, whatever our circumstances, because God will not reach down and change those circumstances however hard we pray, however much we seek to fulfil whatever conditions of prayer we may set up for ourselves or others.

Our loving Heavenly Father knows what we need before ever we ask and will provide for us in his own good time, through the exigencies of life and through others, as our trust in Him grows, but the mechanistic view of prayer is to be completely dispelled if that is to happen and it can only happen as we follow Jesus' example and learn to pray as he taught us. To this we will now turn.

I like to think Jesus may have expected his disciples to have heard his teaching on prayer in the context of his wider ministry and at least after Pentecost, to have been able to put some of the pieces together by understanding that God's way would not be as they might have expected it to be. They might have thought that God's (understandable) wrath would be let loose on His enemies or His own faithless people, but instead, God's covenant fulfilment with all peoples and indeed with all creation, was to be accomplished in and through the sacrificial love of his anointed one, His Christ. He who would take into and upon himself that faithlessness and those projections of wrath, so that once and for all there might be an end to such anger, violence, scapegoating and sacrificial bloodshed and the way opened up to peace, for the whole Earth, for all peoples, towards one another and also within.

After giving them His prayer, Jesus then tells a story, one which prepares the ground for how he wants us to pray in the meantime:

A family was called upon late one night, unexpectedly. Conscious of their responsibility and sacred duty to offer the caller hospitality, but without the means to do so, they turned to a trusted friend in the community to help them out. By the time they called on him it was well past midnight and he and his family were already asleep, the house securely locked. If I were to say to you that sleep is a metaphor for death and the stone was rolled across the entrance to the tomb, perhaps you might get the picture? The one in need, notwithstanding, continued to knock on the householder's door (tomb).

If I were to say that the word translated 'householder', means the one responsible for its entire economy, and that he is a stand in for Almighty God, then once again it might help in understanding that this friend, who can be trusted, understands the need, the late hour and their potential shame in being unable to fulfil a sacred duty. Eventually the householder arises, (I hope I do not have to explicate that word 'arises'), opens the door, (do I need to remind you that Jesus said, I AM the door?) and gives the person *far more* than he needs. He does this not because of the need itself, nor because there is a sacred duty that makes the householder beholden, nor because of the persistence in knocking on that door (as if God's arm could be twisted). He does it because the person is at the end of their rope, without the ability to help themselves. Thus, the answer to the prayer is to do with one qualification and it is this: The person knocking is like the person who finally goes along to an Alcoholics Anonymous Twelve Step meeting for the first time. Such a person is at the end of their rope, they are without ability to help themselves, which they acknowledge, openly, vulnerably, courageously and unashamedly, or possibly shamefully as well, placing themselves in the hands of others and Almighty God who alone can help them. It is helpful to think of this as a picture of how the Church should be, a place where we come with vulnerable, honest hearts, to place ourselves in the hands of God and of others.

And both the answer to this prayer, as well as to the prayer that Jesus gives us, is to be worked out in church, day after day after day. For the answer is not just bread, but far, far more: "For what earthly Father among you will give their child who asks for a fish, a serpent? So, how much more will your Heavenly Father give you, His beloved children, the Holy Spirit when you ask Him!"

The answer to our prayer is the presence of God Himself by his Spirit. The Holy Spirit is the person of God in and to and for all peoples, poured out in fulfilment of Joel's prophecy on the day of Pentecost (Joel 2:28-32/Acts 2:17-21). In the Hebrew Scriptures the word translated Spirit or breath is 'ruach' – a feminine word – thus we might say that She is the answer to our prayers. So we could legitimately say that She will convict us of our inner blindness. She will show us how we are trapped by the false images of ourselves that we present to the world (sin).

That we can dare to trust Her to lead us into the truth, to set us free to trust our Heavenly Father more and more for all our daily needs and to refashion us into the image of his Son, in whom we will experience our truest sense of self. This is the wisdom of the Tree of Life that Adam and Eve so desired in that perfect, beautiful Garden of Eden and it enables us to become like God and to experience a quality and depth to life, called eternal, every new today of our time on Earth, and that is in Her gift.

As you attend church, sit round the table together, break bread, receive the cup of blessing, and with those who, like you, are broken and willing to be outpoured in the service of others, so the answer to your prayer, which is your personal and collective transformation, will emerge in your midst. Remember, when two or three of you gather together there I AM in your midst, furthermore, the alternative Empire, which I came to proclaim and incarnate, is in the midst of you.

So God sent His Holy Spirit, to convict us all of our self-reliance, independence, and self-righteousness, again and again and again. Thus, every new today we can repent, attempt to reconfigure ourselves in the light of our homecoming in God's beloved Son and to stop judging others. We can put aside our desire for self-worth and our sense of security which we get by comparing ourselves to others in judgement and instead have the eyes of our hearts opened to what Jesus did on that Cross, that tree of life, in taking all our wrath and judgement, self-justification, blindness and self-sufficiency into himself once and for all, that all might live in and out of the grace and mercy of Jesus' Heavenly Father.

But this is always going to be really difficult, because to be separated from our sense of self, to die to ego, to crucify the flesh, or anything which is resistant to God's abounding love and grace, will always be a humiliating experience. That's why those on the AA 12-step programme need the other members of the group and their sponsors, because without each other, it is too easy to fall away, and in church, in the same way, we need each other, otherwise it is too easy to stop looking into the mirror of God's grace, which only and always seeks our good; it is too easy to continue to practise that image of a condemnatory God and that familiar image of self, which, we tell ourselves, has always worked well, but which in crisis must fail us.

So, I hope I have already said enough to alert you to the very first word of this prayer, it is not "My" but "Our". It is always about us, not me, and not my, but ours. For Almighty God has no favourites. We are all his beloved children, even though he may show some bias to those with special needs, those who would otherwise be marginalised, the least, the last, the lost. So with this very first word, we are called to remember that all peoples on Earth are children of the same Heavenly Father and are our brothers and sisters and yes, we do have some responsibility towards and for one another!

Similarly, we are not praying to some distant, angry, hard-hearted, legalistic judge, who is either unaware of his children's needs before they pray or unconcerned about them. It is tragic that this view of God is so prevalent and will continue to be so, being manipulated by the religious leaders and guardians of orthodoxy in one generation after another, to maintain a status quo rooted in fear, of a God who is vengeful, angry, violent, and needs to be appeased with the blood of a sacrificial victim.

So let us think of God in a different way – as our Prodigal Father, abounding in steadfast love and faithfulness, who, when rejected by his youngest son, publicly shamed by him and then held at arm's-length by his eldest son for revealing his heart in forgiveness and welcoming home that younger brother, continues to plead with us to drop our guard, let our defences down and come into the heavenly banquet already prepared for us all and indeed already underway, if we only had the ears to hear the sound of the Spirit on the wind.

This Father is utterly to be trusted and to be relied upon to give us all that we need, so that we may be transformed into the image of His Son, into His or Her image bearer, whom we are all called to be on Earth. And whilst earthly fathers may give us a glimpse of our heavenly Father's character, I have witnessed enough in my time on Earth to know that they are not always to be relied upon!

And it is with this experience of our heavenly Father that we must start, for all else flows from this and without the experience of being beloved, all else is the yoke of law, duty and burden. And I am afraid there is no shortcut; indeed –that needs to be broken before it can be remembered, a process which, as I have said, is simply not possible alone. This is why humiliations and suffering are not to be greeted as impostors, but as friends, for they are the doorway into real life in church.

Jesus knew how painful this is. He knew how tempting the broad and easy pathway is when compared to the steep and rugged one, but I hope you will be able to see in His experience of prayer how He wrestled to resist the obvious and easier path and wrestled to continue to put His trust in His Heavenly Father in the wilderness and in the garden of Gethsemane and so throughout His ministry, by taking time out and time alone with His father, so that His orientation might be constantly refocussed.

"So when you pray, say, Our Father in heaven…" Let me reiterate, Heaven is NOT some post-mortem state that some few souls may attain after death, sometime in the future. Heaven is an aspect of our present reality here on Earth that we are asking to experience in our daily lives, our communities, our institutions and our world. For Gentiles the challenge of this was even greater, so let me paint in the background: Moses was asked to construct the Tabernacle in the wilderness, Solomon the Temple in Jerusalem, according to its heavenly model, which was being replicated structurally on Earth. This was so that not simply the *actions* of the High Priest, (in taking the sacrificial blood into the Holy of Holies, and then sprinkling the blood of that animal when once he had emerged in the Temple), but the very building itself, replicated just what it is that occurs in Heaven and that now (once the veil of Christ's flesh had been torn from top to bottom) permeates the whole of the Temple, representing the *whole* of the visible creation.

One day of the year, the High Priest was called upon to enter the Holy of Holies. This represented day one, Heaven, before and outside time. And when he emerged from Heaven, the Holy of Holies, back into the Temple, he was greeted with the cry, "Blessed is He who comes, bearing the NAME, the LORD". Now, Jesus himself has fulfilled that great at-one-ment of all peoples and all things. He has renewed all creation, breathing peace and forgiveness upon all, for all have fallen short of the glory of God. Thus Jesus is presented to us in the New Testament as the great I AM, as both sacrificial victim and High Priest, the creator of all things, both in Heaven, the invisible creation represented by the Holy of Holies, and on Earth, the visible creation represented by the rest of the Temple building.

Jesus has brought eternity into time, and a heavenly reality, or reign of justice and peace, which He calls 'Kingdom', upon Earth. And that Kingdom is therefore, as I say, in the very midst of us, always and everywhere present, so we are praying to live in the present, and in the light of that presence, so that our awareness might go on and on being increased day after every today of his grace, mercy and love towards us all and for His entire creation.

I believe that because the word has been translated 'Kingdom' it has largely been misunderstood throughout the history of the Church. The underlying Greek word meant 'Empire' in Jesus' day. Jesus proclaimed and incarnated an alternative to the Roman Empire with which the Judaism of

His day had become so compromised. That Empire was founded upon and maintained by the myth of redemptive violence. The peace established thereby, known as Pax Romana, only came as a result of the shedding of the blood of others. But in Jesus' alternative empire, animal sacrificial blood or the bloodshed of warfare are not the way to peace. Jesus is fully and finally revealed as the sacrificial lamb slain once and for all. When Jesus declares on the Cross "It is finished", that is precisely what he means, no more bloodshed. It is now clear that that was never the way to lasting peace. So when we pray, "Your Kingdom come", it should be clear that we are praying that this alternative Heavenly Empire will be manifest here and now, on Earth!

Jesus did not say this would be easy and acknowledged that we might struggle to understand what this eternal Heavenly reality would be like in time and space; it is the sixth day of the week when God saw all that he had made and declared it to be very good; it is every experience of the goodness of all things, the wonder, the beauty, the joy, the pleasure, the sense of connectedness of all things. It is also that first Good Friday; the cry of the Psalmist, 'My God, my God, why have you forsaken me?' It is the agony, despair, acute loneliness, pain, suffering and disorientation of all things.

That heavenly reality in which and for which you pray, are those glimpses, those moments of deep connection, within, with one another, with all peoples and with the created order itself, both invisible and visible. It is the intuited sense of the at-one-ment of all things and all peoples in Him who holds all things together in Himself, by his broken body and blood outpoured. And that same Lord prays for us, that our hearts may be opened to see the reality of heaven in our midst, within which we are all deeply embedded.

So when we say; "Our Father in Heaven, Holy be your Name…" we are praying that God's name be made Holy, remarkably, in and through us! For as a result of all that Jesus has done in Heaven, in the Holy of Holies, on the Cross on day one, and in the entire creation, holiness is transferrable through Him and through us to all peoples and to all things.

So now, in Christ, nothing and no one is unclean, none are to be marginalised, excluded or judged, for all in Christ are ransomed, healed, restored, forgiven. No-one is to be turned away from his heavenly banqueting table, all may now draw near, for all are welcome at that table. It is the Lord's Table and any who want to can meet him there.

So then perhaps Jesus' words may have continued something like this:

"When you pray, say, Our Father in Heaven, Holy be your name, your alternative Empire come… that alternative Empire which I incarnated and proclaimed as an *alternative* to that of Rome, which was built on slavery, violence, warfare and injustice. So yes, it is political, yes it is public truth, yes it is the corridors of power, for which you pray, and that Kingdom is in your midst, it emanates from within you to those around you and to the institutions you all inhabit and it is present in these very institutions, however corrupted, for they too are created and redeemed by God."

"And when you pray, say, your will, not my will be done on Earth as it is in Heaven…. Let the heavenly reality of which you are a part and which I have accomplished, be evident in your midst as you sit and eat together, so that you might be salt rubbed into this wounded and decaying world that God so loves and that you may be the light that this dark world so desperately needs. Pray that the sectarianism and legalism that has so come to characterise the people of God, may never creep back into your churches. They are not exclusive clubs with membership qualifications. The only qualification is to come to the point of acknowledging your weakness and need."

"Pray that you may all be ready to serve and to be served, that you may all be willing to love not only your friends, but also and especially those whom you find the most difficult, because it is they, above all, who will reveal to you what you most dislike in yourself. It is the people that you find the most difficult, whom you seek to avoid, who will be holding up a mirror to your dark side, so that you may put away that darkness and be enabled to become your truer, fuller self, the self your Heavenly Father always intended you should become. Pray that you may be open to God's will, take up your cross and follow in my footsteps, in the way that leads to the death of your ego and fullness here and now, of eternal, Heavenly, resurrection life."

"Pray that together you may echo in word and deed, and especially in song, that Heavenly harmony and acclamation of the Heavenly host: Holy, Holy, Holy is the LORD, here on Earth. Pray that you may be ready and willing to encourage one another to use all your resources, all your powers, all your abilities unstintingly in the service of your King, your brother, your friend, since this is the way that leads to peace, shalom and wellbeing for all peoples and all things and especially for those whom the world despises."

"And when you pray, ask your Heavenly Father: Give us today our daily bread... not that there is insufficient bread to feed those who today and tomorrow will go hungry. You can never pray this prayer without being aware of the needs of your brothers and sisters, who, for the lack of justice, for which they also hunger, do not have bread on their tables. Your Father has provided well for all his children's earthly needs, so pray that you will work hard together, so that that bread may be shared the more equitably."

"And when you pray, ask that your Heavenly father will forgive you your debts as you forgive the debts others owe you. For my people were never supposed to lend and charge interest. (According to the book of Leviticus, the 50th year of Jubilee was always supposed to have been the year when all debts were cancelled and when all slaves were released from bondage and all family members returned to the land of their inheritance. In the synagogue in Nazareth at the very beginning of Jesus' public ministry, He declared the fulfilment of the year of Jubilee). So pray for Jubilee in your midst, right here right now today and every day. That you might be released from the debt of the burden of your guilt and shame, and that you might progressively learn to pass that liberation on to your brothers and sisters, and that together you might have the courage and faithfulness to continue to do so."

"And pray this: Lead us not into temptation... of some minor moral individualistic or sexual indiscretion with which the Church habitually gets so tangled up, but rather the temptation to blindness with which you are all afflicted, such that you cannot see yourselves or others as you truly are. Do not let reward and punishment, judgemental attitudes, self-justification and blame take you over."

"And then finally pray... but deliver us from the evil one..... For he so wants to mislead you, to distract you and to cause you all to stumble along the way. But do not fear, for underneath are the everlasting arms in which your Heavenly Father will catch you. And never fear if you do wander off, as you assuredly will, because I AM, the Good Shepherd and I will bring you home on my shoulders rejoicing. Pray that you may not listen to his accusations and his lies that would undermine your security in your status as the beloved children of your Heavenly Father. Pray that he would not deceive you into believing that your Heavenly Father's love is to be earned or that it may be denied or that it can ever be limited. Nothing can ever separate you from God, for He *is* Love."

In his letter to the church in Pergamum at the beginning of the book of Revelation, using metaphorical language, Jesus brings His judgement through the sharp two-edged sword in his mouth. This sword separates us, as children of God, from the flesh, which symbolises our individual resistance to the good and gracious purposes of God in our lives. In just the same way, this sword will separate us from our collective resistance to the good and gracious purposes of God, represented as it is by the city, which must, whether it be Babylon or Jerusalem, be destroyed, so that we may become dwellers in that new Garden City that is descended from Heaven. This is a place wherein there are no more tears, a place where there is no more mourning, no more death, for God has made all things new in Him who cried as he did it, "It is accomplished!" For now the dwelling of God is with all peoples and the gates of that city are forever open, so that the wealth and accomplishments of the nations may be gathered in.

What a vision! Furthermore, in his letter to the church in Laodicea, Jesus offers people salve for their blind eyes, so that they may be enabled to see themselves as He sees them. They think they are self-sufficient, well-dressed and rich; he views them as poor, blind and naked. He offers to clothe them in His righteousness, so that they may see themselves and their neighbours as He sees them- as interdependent, beloved image bearers, who may overcome, by their own self-sacrificial laying down of their egos, as He did before them. And this is His alternative Empire established on Earth and His will accomplished on Earth, as it is done in Heaven.

So let us pray that we may be enabled to return again and again to the essentials outlined in this book and be re-membered in Jesus, put back together with the awareness of who we all truly are, for none of us can manage on our own; the allure of the flesh and the city will prevail. We need one another if we are to become an alternative to the assembly of the city and the assembly of the synagogue, to be an authentic church. Let us pray that we may be enabled to say, "I am not okay", and to hear others respond liturgically, "No, and I am not okay either", and then to say together, "We are not okay"… and then to hear God respond, "But you are all okay. For I am your loving Heavenly Father, My grace is abundant, prodigal and so much more than sufficient."

And so to the conclusion: "For the Kingdom, the power and the glory are yours now and for ever, Amen." This alternative Empire extends to the four corners of the Earth and it is a Heavenly Empire. It extends back in what we call time and forwards to embrace all of what you will call history, but which one day you shall see is but His story. This alternative Empire is everywhere present, dwells within us, has already been accomplished, is waiting to be revealed and is ours to establish on Earth together by the power that is at work within us. For it is His power that is at work within this world and perhaps the more remarkably, within us all. So then let us strive to work out the shape of that alternative Empire, wherever it is that we find ourselves to have been placed, by the hand of Almighty God our Heavenly Father.

And not only is it His Heavenly Empire and His almighty power, but it is to His glory. The glory which is ultimately revealed on the Cross is made perfect in us as we are released from our bondage to self, as we allow ourselves to be seen to be vulnerable, as we participate in church together and find that by the power of his love between us, we are refashioned into his image bearers, making us strong, even when we are weak. So let us pray that we may participate in the sufferings of Christ and that thus we may know the power of the love of God at work among us; that as we are broken and share our brokenness, we may find again and again that it feels as if, in being poured out, we experience the very life of God in our midst, in our communities, in our institutions and in our world, and most especially as we sit eat at this table together.

Amen and Amen.

Conclusion

I do not intend to summarise what I have explored throughout this book. What I do want to do however, is to make some comment about two glaring omissions in Luke's one verse summary of that to which the early Church devoted itself, because their absence is especially significant and Luke's silence deafening. Where, we must ask, is their commitment to mission, or their focus on worship?

In our day, even corporate giants regard it as normal to have a mission statement. Every Anglican parish is required by its Diocese to have one. And every Anglican church is required to order its worship according to canon law. In these days of declining church attendance, the institutional church is prioritising mission. Even if, and perhaps this is overly cynical, it is only on the purely pragmatic grounds that more 'bums on pews' means more income and a maintained status quo for another generation.

In the commercial field, considerable attention is given to advertising, marketing, and product quality and delivery. Only thinly veiled, the same is true within the religious sphere, with each church here in Cambridge for example, very conscious of the competition for what seems like an ever dwindling market share. Thus the professionalism, quality and content of the worship 'service', together with the organisation and infrastructure surrounding it, is critical for perceived success, gauged in the number of religious consumers attending services each week, for which endless local and national statistics are produced.

So why the silence in the early Church? Why do their priorities seem so different to ours? In this book, we have explored their four-fold devotion, which resulted in mushrooming numbers of revivalist proportions in the church. We have undertaken this review in the conviction that a return to their type of devotion might serve the church in and of our day rather better than its current priorities and preoccupations.

Of course those who gathered then (Ecclesia), were doing so in the Temple (Luke 24:53), where they, together with their Jewish brethren (excluding their Jewish sisterhood of course), met for worship. And whilst there would have been some 'Godfearers', Gentile converts to Judaism among them, the vast majority were Jews by birth, and therefore members of a religion exclusive by definition, whose membership is rooted in its ethnicity, and for whom there is no missional impetus whatsoever, it being a closed loop, determined by bloodline and purity concerns, rather than by either behaviour or belief.

Thus, at its birth, this early Church continued to participate in the exclusively male and Jewish 'worship' in the Temple without any thought of a missional calling beyond itself. They did so with the ardent hope that God's elect, God's ancient people, the children of Israel, would, post-resurrection, recognise that in the crucifixion of Jesus, 'they' had participated in the killing of the Christ, whom God had promised to them, God's anointed Son, the suffering servant of Isaiah. They ardently hoped that their Jewish brethren would acknowledge that this same Jesus was also the one who had anthropomorphised 'God most high' throughout their history, in the person of the LORD.

However, this anticipated and expected recognition was not forthcoming, and the need to work out an alternative form for, as well as location of, their 'worship', became necessary, as the sense grew that they were being viewed not as the fulfilment of their own religion and of God's purposes, but as a somewhat annoying minority sect within the religion of their birth. At the same time as they found themselves being pushed out and indeed persecuted by their fellow Jews, they also found that unclean Gentiles were being added to their number. This only added to the challenges they faced if they were to be able to gather together.

The Temple, therefore, became an increasingly impossible context for such a mixed company, as did the form of gathering that had taken the name 'synagogue', dominated as it was by male participation and leadership, coupled with the segregation of women and the exclusion of various categories of those deemed to be unclean.

As these egalitarian gatherings of those with mixed backgrounds, differing ethnicities and status began to emerge, they were required to meet in the few homes of those with the means to host such gatherings, which lead over time to a brand new economy called (ecclesia) – 'church emerging'. The name church was deliberately chosen, as we have seen, as one of two words used to describe the gatherings of God's ancient people in the Hebrew Scriptures, whom they wanted to express their continuity with, yet at the same time, their distinctiveness from.

The other word used in the Hebrew Scriptures for the gathering together of God's people was synagogue. But this was the name by which the Jews in their day were known and was not therefore appropriate. For the gatherings of Jews in both synagogue and Temple were rooted in, and upholders of, the Mosaic law, with its separation from the world, its male domination, its clear lines of segregation and concerns with purity, which had resulted in so many, even of their own ethnicity, being excluded from said gatherings, because of an uncleanness that Jesus completely ignored..

Thus from its earliest origins and beginnings, these new gatherings were characterised by a very mixed and inclusive economy, in which not only could male Jews and male Gentiles mix, but they could do so alongside female Jews and female Gentiles. And they did so in the homes of their elite hosts, who were learning to participate on an equal footing with their slaves. Nothing like this had ever been witnessed before. It was neither permissible within polite society, which was highly stratified, nor within the Judaism of their day, which was similarly stratified, highly sectarian and exclusive, as I have said.

I hope it has been made clear what an extremely radical departure this was from the religion of their birth, which would unravel and be worked out in the years that followed. For even to use the word 'mix' was utterly to fly in the face of the Levitical purity code that was so central to their Jewish identity and religious practice, and for whom such mixing was a complete taboo. In time, of course, these innovative social gatherings would require theological interpretation which would become what we now have recorded for us in the New Testament, and would become known as 'church'.

So it is also worth noting at this point three things that can easily be overlooked. First, this new thing initiated by the Holy Spirit, was not simply egalitarian, as radical as that was, but was also, right from its inception, and by definition, an open, inclusive and a universally representative gathering. Although as we have traced, it would fall foul of religious institutionalism, restrictive laws, entry requirements and exclusive clauses, this was not so at its beginning. It was then, as it is called to be still, non-sectarian, non-judgemental, unrestrictive and welcoming of all, whatever creed, race, belief, gender, or sexual orientation. It was called to be a representation on Earth of the multi-national gathering around the throne in heaven (Rev. 7:9).

Stephen bore witness to this and was stoned for blasphemy (Acts 7). He said that he had seen the Son of Man, on the right hand side of the throne of God most High, the one who had revealed himself in the history of His people, on Earth and in time and space, as Yahweh, the Lord. Not only was such a vision disallowed, but the title 'Son of Man' had been THE title that Jesus deliberately and allusively took to Himself whilst on Earth, that which Peter affirmed and proclaimed that first Pentecost.

This was the Son of Man, whom New Testament theologians would later understand as THE full, final, and complete revelation, not only of the divine, but of the human. 'Christianity' as it would become known, was never just another exclusive religion with its own set of rules, beliefs and practices, but rather was a gathering of those seeking to follow in the footsteps of Jesus and become more and more fully human. It was a gathering of those who were stumblingly aware of how far short they had all fallen.

It could not therefore legitimately exclude anyone, for *all* have fallen short; nor judge anyone, for *all* are judged; nor elevate some over others, for *all* are equally graced and equally beloved – indeed, all are human. All peoples are created good, thus all people are those within whom the light of Christ resides from their birth and upon whom the Spirit of the living God has been breathed, not just those members of the 'chosen' race, as had been previously understood. And at the same time, all peoples are also broken, failing, and resistant to God's purposes within themselves, capable of the darkest motives, words and actions, and most definitely mortal, defiant and hostile towards the eternity set deep within their hearts (Eccl. 3:11).

'Christianity' then was never in its essence a new religion, but rather an original, now re-established and always intended, way of being human. Endeavouring to follow the teaching of Jesus who encourages his followers to treat others NOT as they have been treated, but as they would like to be treated, He calls us to break the cycle of 'tit for tat', with an outworking of generosity, gentleness, kindness, and good neighbourliness.

Endeavouring to follow His example, His manner of life, and in the manner of His death, Jesus calls a person to be willing not to respond to violence in like manner, but to be willing to be made a scapegoat of and for the violence of others, that all might 'see' that non-violent resistance of injustice and the abuse of power, is the way to life and peace. As Gandhi famously said, 'An eye for an eye will leave the whole world blind'.

Second, this early group of confused disciples stumbling towards an understanding of what it was that had happened to them and in their world, were entrusted to be able, together, to work it out. I remember years ago listening to a preacher who started his sermon by saying, "Don't believe a word I say, trust yourself to the inner resonance between whatever you are hearing and the Holy Spirit's inner confirmation thereof." He was charismatic in every sense of that word, a great orator, band-leader, singer/songwriter, and all round long-haired cool 'dude', but what he was suggesting was that we together, and together with the Holy Spirit, could be trusted to work this all out for ourselves and that we did not need a patriarchal authority set over us.

This was as radical when I heard it as it was when Jesus left his disciples to work it out and as it was when the Holy Spirit overwhelmed all those that first Pentecost and entrusted them to work out its implications together. The idea that human beings could be trusted without the aid of rules and regulations, law, patriarchy, authority and bureaucracy, to work out their salvation, this new way of being together, was frightening then to those so called, and is just as threatening to the guardians of institutional religion now.

There is a variety of contexts in which human beings gather together – companies, schools, councils, families, churches – institutions which enable human beings to accomplish a whole variety of important, normal, everyday, good purposes, intended to be for the benefit of all. But whilst such institutions may pay lip service to the idea of transparency, of all voices being heard and considered, to the ideal of mutual trust and compromise, generally speaking, that it all it is, lip service. Most institutions, in my experience, are top down organisations, with the most powerful persons and voices having status, generally male. The Church is no different, and falls woefully short of the fourfold devotion and aspiration of the early Church. But Jesus forged egalitarian trust and mutuality amongst those he gathered around Him and in His name, anticipating that, through the Holy Spirit, this would be the reality after his Ascension.

The third is that theology always follows experience and the reverse is not only *not* true, (not for the early Church nor in my own experience over many years), but can also be very dangerous, bordering on indoctrination and fanaticism. It is dangerous, not simply for those who almost inevitably end up being the targets of such authoritarian, episcopal, bureaucratic or institutional abuse, but also for those required to believe what does not cohere with their life experience, causing a disjunction between the reality of their experience and their theoretical belief systems.

It is, I would say, just one of the causes in the West, of so many losing their confidence in the institutional church, which is viewed as hypocritical, out of touch and irrelevant in, to and for the real world, where people actually live. This was most certainly NOT the case for this nascent sect who grew in favour, not only with God, but with their neighbours (Acts 2:47).

I well remember as a young cleric listening to a highly respected older preacher telling us, "You must never allow your experience to affect or alter your theology". This advice, it seems to me, was dangerous for us who, in a variety of ways would find that what we had thought was a theological framework for life and ministry, turned out to be significantly flawed and in need of constant revision through our lives. In passing, how absurd to think that what I believed about anything at the age of 30, let alone about God, would be what I would believe at the age of 60!

But how dangerous for this older preacher also, for many years later, it became known how flawed he was and how his personal experience was at considerable variance with his professed and proclaimed beliefs. How sad for him and how tragic that the Church, of all gatherings, which too often sells out to this theoretical and cerebral way of viewing self and others, has so lost track of its inner birth right and trust in the Holy Spirit and the truth, that as the old hymn, *Through All the Changing Scenes of Life* affirms, "experience will decide", whether we find we like that truth or not, and whether that truth coheres with what we have always liked to say we think we believe, or not.

We are called, as the Church, to trust that inner resonance, one another and the Holy Spirit, and not to allow ourselves to become infantilised by authoritative leaders who, just like us, are sheep that have gone astray and need to be brought home on the Good Shepherd's shoulders again and again. I remember too attending my first clergy conference after ordination and seeing through the veneer of what had been presented to me, in my local church, as the authority of the ordained leadership – somehow holier, more trustworthy, and closer to God… Nonsense!

With all that having been said, let us return to the strange omissions of worship and mission from Luke's summary record. For it does seem strange to us as modern day Western readers, that neither are central to the life, ministry and purpose of the early Church and this, it seems to me, requires some further comment.

I think there are a number of reasons for this. First, and as we have already alluded to, the makeup of the early Church would have been in the main from the wrong end of the social spectrum. Just as when Jesus was on Earth the appeal of the Gospel, the good news of God's grace to all, freely given, unconditionally, no strings attached, was far, far greater to those with nothing to lose, than ever it was to those with much to lose. The rich young ruler, who in the world's eyes had everything, was left sad after his encounter with Jesus. Jesus observes that it would be easier for a camel to go through the eye of a needle than for a rich person to enter (Luke 18:25) into the quality of life, namely this earthly life with an eternal or Heavenly dimension, that Jesus proclaimed and incarnated. This world's riches, far from being a sign of God's blessing are, according to Jesus, a major stumbling block.

My experience, limited though it is, of visiting communities associated with projects that our little church supports in other, poorer parts of the planet, together with those occasions when I have accompanied a friend to an AA meeting, are very suggestive in this regard. The depth, quality and reality of acceptance, welcome, hospitality and lack of judgement, as well as an innate sense of the honour attributable to another human being just because they are that a human being, rooted in a shared experience of suffering, lack, pain, exclusion and judgement, bears eloquent witness to the truth of these words with which Jesus began his public ministry: "Blessed are the poor in Spirit for theirs is the alternative Empire of heaven" (Matt. 5:3).

Financial security, material wellbeing, social infrastructure, legal, educational and health care provision and so much more, are all the immense benefits of capitalism and industrialisation that Western civilisation enjoys, but as the Beatles sang all those years ago, *"Money Can't Buy Me Love"*, a truth that we all know, even if we don't live by it. If such benefits as these lead to virtue signalling, pretension, a sense of superiority, the need to wear a mask of success and the inability for shame to be personally revealed to another, then what Jesus empowered those on the margins to step out into and celebrate with Him, in the Hebrew tradition termed "Shalom" and in the African, "Abuntu", will, paradoxically, always be stumbling blocks to life in all its fullness, that Western civilisation promises, but so evidentially fails to deliver.

The early Church, made up as it mainly was, from those who had none of these benefits, but rather those who were oppressed, disempowered, marginalised, without status, financial ability or security, was simply the company of those liberated into an expression of being able to celebrate together their shared experience of the status given them in, through and by Jesus. Whilst their circumstances had not changed whatsoever, as those living on the underside of polite society, nonetheless, everything within them – their sense of self, their view of others, their confidence in the purposes of God and his way of working in the world, with the least the last and the lost, had changed for ever. That was their experience and their legacy.

Thus, for those on the margins in the poorer parts of the world and those finding they cannot hide their addictions from others any longer, such an expression of that shared identity, need, belovedness, acceptance, grace and blessing, is just as available today as then. However it is much less likely to be found in churches made up of those who enjoy all the material benefits this world has to offer than where those benefits are lacking. The popularity of this Gospel was and is always going to be amongst those who know that they are on the bottom rung of society's ladder. Those who unashamedly dare to step out into the light of Christ, and who through the cracks in their lives, allow that light within them to connect in and through others with the love, compassion, forgiveness, grace and mercy of Jesus.

It was the case then, and will now I believe still be the case, that radical, egalitarian, authentic gatherings, without judgement, that are honest and vulnerable, will be the place of such connection and encounter. Those who dare to join such a company on those terms, will be blessed. Those who have much to lose will not want to join such company today any more than they did then. Such gatherings are self-recommending.

Their 'worship' was imminent, in that it authentically connected them with their own humanity and that of other human beings. And it was transcendent, in that it connected them with the divinity within them and others and beyond themselves. It was this that I experienced in my overseas visits and attendance at AA meetings with my friend, and that so powerfully moved me. And that experience, that movement in my heart or my soul is, I would say, a genuine missional outcome.

Luke witnessed the truth of this and thus there is no need for, nor mention of, mission or worship. The reality and authenticity of their gatherings outworked in their communal lives would have been self-evident to their neighbours. And the decline in church 'attendance' in the West has much to do with the lack of authenticity of such gatherings and such 'attendance', having become congregational consumerism, with attendees not needing to get their hands dirty, whilst paid staff are on hand to do their dirty work, the core values of the alternative Empire of Jesus, their service in the world, of their neighbour, the stranger and even their enemy, as explicated by Jesus' parable of the Good Samaritan, (Luke 10:25-37), being reduced to a 'service' on a Sunday morning, and the job of paid employees.

In that early Church therefore such missional outcomes were only the fruit of their worship, namely their daily lives offered in service back to God (Rom. 12:1) and gathered up as and when they met. As they devoted themselves to those things that we have explored in this book, so the Lord added to their number, but – and this is a huge but – that was his concern and not theirs! Nevertheless it was utterly inevitable as a result of their faithfulness and fourfold devotion. And the extent to which we do the same, so shall it be true of the Church in our day.

But living as we do in the West at such material advantage, makes it extremely challenging to incarnate service of this kind when we all have so much to lose. The necessity to put aside our masks and be seen as at an A. A. meeting, is generally too much to ask and too much of a risk. As a result, the Church in our day is too often reduced to some form of marketing strategy, which is only ever going to be as 'successful' as its commercial counterpart, to which it has sold out and upon which it is tragically modelled. A return to the model of that early Church is the only way; we must go backwards if we genuinely wish to go forwards.

We have explored in some depth the major reason why it is not recorded by Luke that the early Church prioritised either worship or mission. We might express this another way and say positively that this was because their entire lives were lived sacrificially, which was, as they understood it, their worship, and by such service, so too was it missional.

Before we draw things to a close, there are one or two other things that we need to say. The early Church, as is clear in the Letters now included within the body of the New Testament, expected Jesus' imminent return, and thus there was no need for mission. The expectation was that God's ancient people would respond to their Messiah, who would return and gather the nations around Him and his people in Jerusalem, rendering 'mission' unnecessary.

Furthermore, the continuing persecution of the early Church by the religion that had given it birth, meant that the attention of that early Church was not on mission but on survival, which the book of Acts testifies resulted in a missional outcome. Perhaps this can be likened to the situation in China, when Western missionaries were thrown out in the 1950s crackdown. After the communist lockdown came to an end, those Christians who returned, discovered not only that this oppressed, persecuted and under-resourced Church, without Western leadership, had survived, but that it had actually increased in number and was thriving.

The focus of attention in a minority sect is very different from that of an established 'majority' religion. Only centuries later with the 'conversion' of the Emperor Constantine would 'Christianity' as it could then become known, become another established religion in its own right. As a result, and all too predictably, this once persecuted minority sect, once it had assumed power, became guilty of anti-Semitism, the Crusades, and perhaps even worse, the conquest of the majority of the world in the name of Christ, resulting in the massacre of millions of indigenous 'savages', and all regarded as its legitimate 'mission'!

That early Church however, which would remain a persecuted minority within the Judaism of its day, would only finally have a sense of itself as an alternative thereto, with the destruction of the Temple in Jerusalem. Their focus was very much upon not providing any further cause for offence than was necessary and alongside their fellow Jews, avoiding provoking the Roman authorities further. Their neighbourliness and sacrificial service in their communities gave them a reputation for goodness and kindness, which inevitably increased their number.

Finally then, their expectation of Jesus' imminent return was focussed in their understanding of the centrality of Jerusalem and its Temple, to God's purposes. As a result, it was only persecution by their fellow Jews which forced them to disperse from Jerusalem and Judea, through Samaria and to the ends of the Earth. Only much later still, as it was to be recorded by Luke, would the Church begin to see and acknowledge its resistance to what it turned out was God's purpose all along, namely, to include Gentiles as well as Jews within His covenant.

Therefore, the word mission would have been, in those early days, simply anachronistic! The Lord's return was expected, the ingathering of the nations to Jerusalem and primacy of God's ancient elect people, were all central tenets of the established faith that was giving birth to this new 'messianic sect'. Thus the very idea that God's purposes in salvation would include Gentiles, was all too painful, too impossible and still some way from landing in their consciousness. And to say that there is an emphasis on 'evangelism' in the New Testament is not only anachronistic, but would be to read what is simply not there, since the word 'evangelism' is never used.

I want to end this book by quoting a piece that I was sent when I first came here to St Paul's, Cambridge, as vicar in 1993. It had been written by a former pastor and good friend of a friend of mine and has been something of an inspiration and guiding light to me ever since. It attempts to encapsulate what it is that I think the verse we have been exploring seeks to affirm.

The fellowship of those who are devoted to the mystical food of Jesus' flesh and blood outpoured and the reinterpretation of the Hebrew Scriptures, as recorded by the Apostles and directed by the Holy Spirit, upon whom they seek to be dependent in prayer, will inevitably find itself to be a missio-logical worshipping community that is attractive to those not yet of their number, who at the very least are curious about such an alternative way of being, on their doorstep.

"I have a vision of a church whose worship seeks out all the resources of its members and utilises all their skills. Where the hymns are sung with zest, perception and expression, and accompanied by every instrument anyone can play, including hands and feet and smiles. And where the unfamiliar music of another generation is learned until it is loved.

A church with liturgies that are never mechanical, and spontaneity that is never trivial. Where the best meetings are conducted like royal appointments, and its greatest days are marked with solemn hilarity. Where organisational efficiency is always at the service of caring love. Where even poor efforts are done with painstaking diligence, and commended with tolerant hope.

Where brilliance of mind or skill only serves to light up Jesus Christ and his Gospel, where no one can hog the limelight, no one gets too much attention, and no one gets left out. Of a church where outsiders get as much welcome as old friends, where no-one stands alone unless they need to, where the awkward ones are accepted, and the pleasant ones are disturbed by hard realities. Where the first to hear a complaint is the offender, and the last to air it is the sufferer. Where people's interests are worldwide, without being worldly, and personal without being petty.

I have a vision of a church which shares an invincible passion for learning and giving, whose life is energised by a glad acceptance of the Cross as a way of life. Whose self-critical humour puts people at ease, and whose self-denials disturb and embrace them. Whose sympathy is so warm and imaginative that no one has the nerve to indulge in self-pity, and whose ideals are so high that slightly soiled notions are shamed into silence. Whose convictions are firm without being rigid, whose tolerance extends even to the intolerant, whose life is admonition, whose love learns even from its opponents, and whose faith is infectious.

I have a vision of a church that is like that because from time to time it hears its Redeemer's voice speak with such authority that nothing will do but obedience, nothing matters but God's love, and others coming in can only wonder, and wish, and ask..."

(John R Peck, Mch 1979, Earl Soham, Suffolk).